C000063310

# EXTRAORDINARY BRITISH TRANSFERWARE: 1780-1840

ROSEMARY HALLIDAY
&
RICHARD HALLIDAY

4880 Lower Valley Road • Atglen, PA 19310

This book is dedicated to the many potters that produced the wares that we all love, collect, deal in, write about, and adore.

Copyright © 2012 by Rosemary & Richard Halliday

Library of Congress Control Number: 2012937458

All rights reserved. No part of this work may be reproduced or used in any form or by any means—graphic, electronic, or mechanical, including photocopying or information storage and retrieval systems—without written permission from the publisher.

The scanning, uploading and distribution of this book or any part thereof via the Internet or via any other means without the permission of the publisher is illegal and punishable by law. Please purchase only authorized editions and do not participate in or encourage the electronic piracy of copyrighted materials.

"Schiffer," "Schiffer Publishing Ltd. & Design," and the "Design of pen and inkwell" are registered trademarks of Schiffer Publishing Ltd.

Designed by Mark David Bowyer
Type set in Trajan Pro / Souvenir Lt BT

ISBN: 978-0-7643-3974-5
Printed in Hong Kong

Schiffer Books are available at special discounts for bulk purchases for sales promotions or premiums. Special editions, including personalized covers, corporate imprints, and excerpts can be created in large quantities for special needs. For more information contact the publisher:

Published by Schiffer Publishing Ltd.
4880 Lower Valley Road
Atglen, PA 19310
Phone: (610) 593-1777; Fax: (610) 593-2002
E-mail: Info@schifferbooks.com

For the largest selection of fine reference books on this and related subjects, please visit our website at
**www.schifferbooks.com**
We are always looking for people to write books on new and related subjects. If you have an idea for a book, please contact us at
proposals@schifferbooks.com

This book may be purchased from the publisher.
Please try your bookstore first.
You may write for a free catalog.

In Europe, Schiffer books are distributed by
Bushwood Books
6 Marksbury Ave.
Kew Gardens
Surrey TW9 4JF England
Phone: 44 (0) 20 8392 8585; Fax: 44 (0) 20 8392 9876
E-mail: info@bushwoodbooks.co.uk
Website: www.bushwoodbooks.co.uk

# Contents

# Foreword

Having been a student and collector of transfer-printed pottery for the past thirty years, I have benefited from the valuable research and publications of many authors whose dedication to the field of British ceramics, the industry and its workers has resulted in numerous books on the subject. While some are scholarly in nature, others are oriented toward the novice, serving to educate and to generate interest in collecting transfer-printed wares. This new book, *Extraordinary British Transferware, 1780-1840,* by the mother and son team, Rosemary and Richard Halliday, addresses the field of transferware with a fresh and intriguing approach; it presents the reader with an incredible selection of rare and highly unusual examples of transferware patterns and shapes found in private collections from around the world.

The authors, fourth and fifth generation antiquarians, have been engaged exclusively for the past eighteen years in buying and selling blue transfer-printed pottery. Active in both the direct trade and in online commerce with their own web site, the Hallidays have established close relationships with a considerable number of advanced collectors, affording them access to private collections enjoyed by only a few privileged colleagues and friends. In this book, with the permission of both customers and colleagues, they enable us to see for the first time a collection of some of the most unusual, scarce, and intriguing examples produced by British potteries between 1780 and 1840. Applying a strict set of criteria for the selection of items to be included in this handsome publication, the authors present us with an extraordinary collection of some of the most desirable and highly sought after transfer-printed pottery items ever seen. They are items that rarely come to market as collectibles and are representative of a broad range of pottery production, including dinner and tea ware items, toilet and medical wares, commemorative, named and dated wares, children's wares, and items used for drink and in the preparation of food.

Organized and presented in an exhibition-like style with outstanding photography, the authors place emphasis on the physical and aesthetic characteristics of each item while providing the basic information concerning the potteries that produced each piece, if known, and the approximate dates of manufactory, dimensions, features, and function.

The Hallidays, as long-standing members of the Transferware Collectors Club (TCC), have supported the TCC Pattern and Source Print Database by providing many patterns for documentation. Richard Halliday also served as photographer and contributing editor for the recently launched Spode Exhibition Online, a joint project of the Transferware Collectors Club, the Winterthur Museum, Garden, and Library, and the Pottery Museum, Stoke-on-Trent. A 2010 recipient of the TCC's Richards Foundation Research Grant for the Study of Transferware, Richard Halliday has only recently published his project titled *Blue Printed Pickle Dishes and Milseys: A Social and Historical Commentary*. This 204-page volume documents the large and one-of-a-kind collection of the late Robin Greeves and provides an interesting social and historical perspective for these two, often misunderstood, forms of transfer-printed British pottery. I am confident that *Extraordinary British Transferware, 1780-1840* will serve as a valuable source of information and enjoyment for transferware collectors and researchers alike.

—Loren L. Zeller, President
Transferware Collectors Club
www.transferwarecollectorsclub.org

# Acknowledgments

This book is primarily made up of the collections of the following people. We are fully aware of the enormous amount of gratitude we owe them all. Simply put, this book would not have been possible without the time, energy, enthusiasm, and hospitality generously donated by them to us.

Tony and Margaret Ashton, Michael and Vicky Attar, David Boyer, Martyn and Sheila Edgell, Sheila and Robert French, Fred Heathcote, Paul and Kath Holdway, John and Nancy Homewood, Leo and Malcolm Leader, Ivan Mears, Nicholas and Pat Moore, Colin and Patricia Parkes, Dave and Judy Pollitt, Peter and Susan Rees, Connie Rogers, Judie Siddall, John and Pat Stanley, Grahame and Arleen Tanner, Nick and Pat Wolstenholme, Loren Zeller, and those who wish to remain anonymous.

# Introduction

What is *Extraordinary British Transferware*? The Oxford Dictionary tells us that *extraordinary* means *"unusual or remarkable; out of the usual course," "unusually great,"* or *"so exceptional as to provoke astonishment or admiration."* This is true in all senses when applied to the contents of this book.

The original working title of the book was *Transferware Rarities*. Whilst this was a good title and did describe the contents well, we felt that the word *rare* is an over-used and often misused term, especially when applied to transferware. Labels such as this are often subjective and trying to define and quantify what this means is extremely difficult. One person's idea of rare may be substantially different to another's. So, we were keen to steer clear of such an ambiguous title that could be open to a great deal of conjecture. As such, we settled on the title *Extraordinary British Transferware, 1780-1840*. We feel that this title best encapsulates what this book is about.

Pieces within this book had to fit the following criteria when we were deciding what should be incorporated. This was our primary check-list for inclusion.

A piece must be:

- **Uncommon:** either in terms of pattern, shape, manufacturer, use, size, or a combination of these factors.
- **Interesting:** either in terms of the history of its use, who it was produced for, why it was produced, or a combination of these points.
- **Thought-provoking:** some items' use is still a mystery and an appearance in a book such as this might lead to answers. After all, this is one of the joys of this subject.

We were very conscious about not producing yet another run-of-the-mill antiques text book. These books definitely do have their place and offer a huge amount of valuable information on their given subjects. However, we wanted to show off these superb pieces of transferware in their best possible light and we believe the best way to achieve this is in photographic form.

We hope that you enjoy this book and that it will serve as an inspiration and will make you look again at the wonderful and diverse subject of transferware with renewed enthusiasm. If you are interested to know about the history of transferware and the social and historical reasons behind its inception, then there are many, very good and informative books on the subject. We suggest that you look at the Bibliography & Recommended Reading section of this book for further information. One particular reference work that should be viewed if you are interested to know about the production of transferware is *Spode Transfer Printed Ware 1784-1833* by David Drakard & Paul Holdway. This has excellent credentials as both Paul Holdway and his father Harold worked at the Spode works as highly-skilled engravers.

Our book is laid out in a very specific and easy-to-use way. Each of the items within this work has one page dedicated to it. This item-specific page will give details of the manufacturer, size and dimensions, marks, and a description. Most importantly though, it will have multiple, high-quality images to best illustrate the piece.

Sizes are provided in both inches and centimetres. They are often rounded up or down to the nearest quarter-inch or half-centimetre.

# Collecting Transferware

One of the great joys of transferware is the sheer diversity within one subject.

There are simply many various ways to collect. You can collect by pattern, by style, by manufacturer, or by time period. You can collect by shape, by size, or by colour. You can collect as an investment or as a decoration, but the best piece of advice we can offer is that you buy what you like and enjoy it.

A really interesting part of writing this book was to see how collectors live with their own collections. Some collectors have pieces as accent marks within a room's decoration. Some have them as pieces of artwork, whereas others have their pieces as living history. Some collectors have pieces dotted around the house and some have rooms dedicated to their collecting. Some have every surface and wall space adorned with transferware. This again beautifully illustrates how collecting transferware is something personal and unique and it is exactly what you want it to be.

One way to look at collecting transferware is that you never actually own a piece; you are merely a temporary custodian of an important historical object. Your job is two-fold: to love and enjoy it and to look after it for future generations. Collecting transferware is a relatively inexpensive way of collecting art if you think about it. If you hang a platter on your wall it is equally as enchanting and pleasing as a painting. Often the patterns are taken directly from paintings or prints so have the right balance and feel to them.

There are no rules within collecting or building up a collection, only those that you impose on yourself. It doesn't matter who you are or how long you have been collecting, there are always new things to see, find out, learn, and share. Two things are guaranteed though: the more you find out and learn, the less you realise you know, and collecting transferware is a drug which is difficult to quit.

We hope you enjoy our book.

—R & R Halliday

Chapter 1

# Food Preparation & Storage

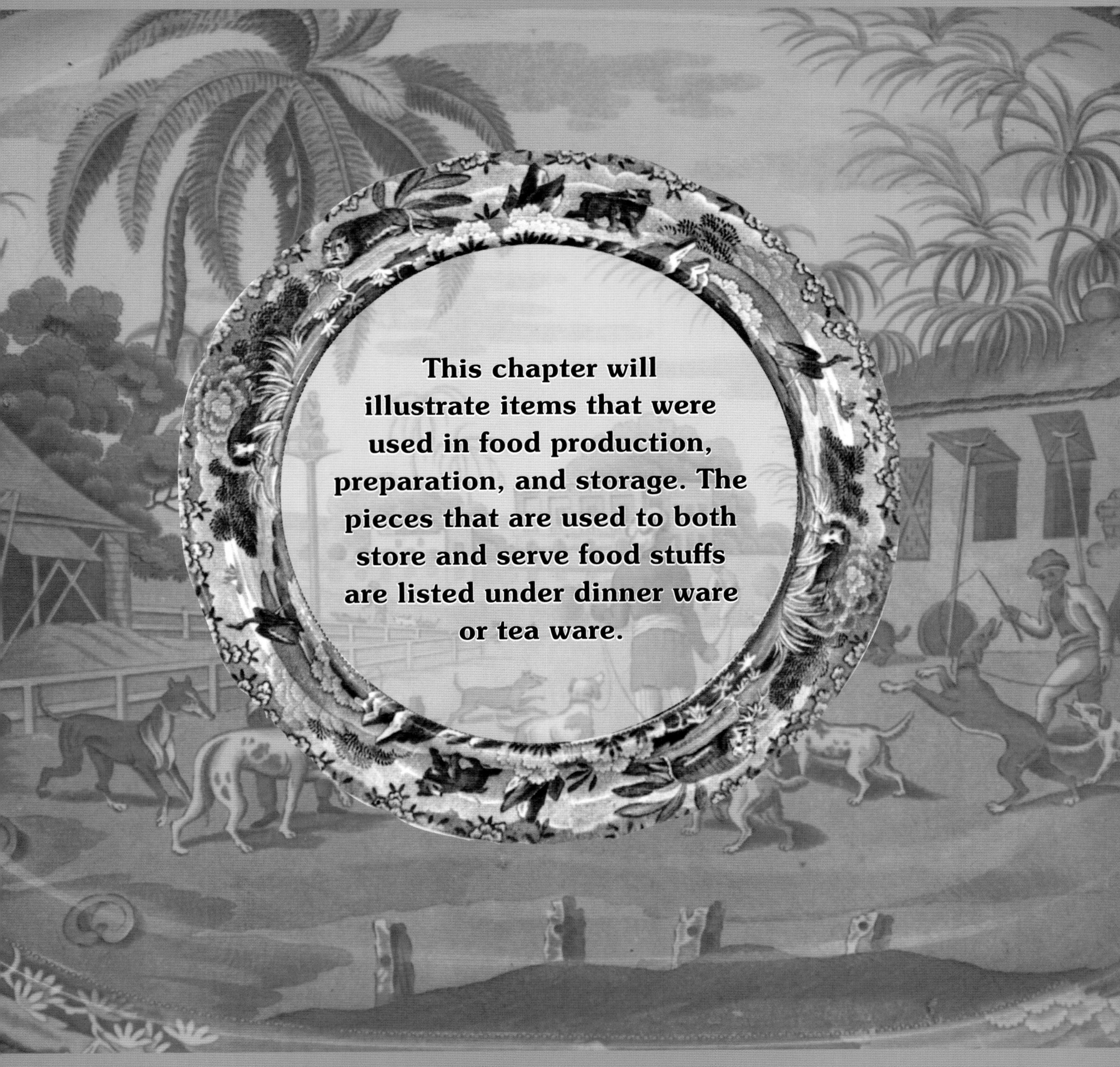

**This chapter will illustrate items that were used in food production, preparation, and storage. The pieces that are used to both store and serve food stuffs are listed under dinner ware or tea ware.**

# Giant Spode Tower Pattern Skimming Bowl

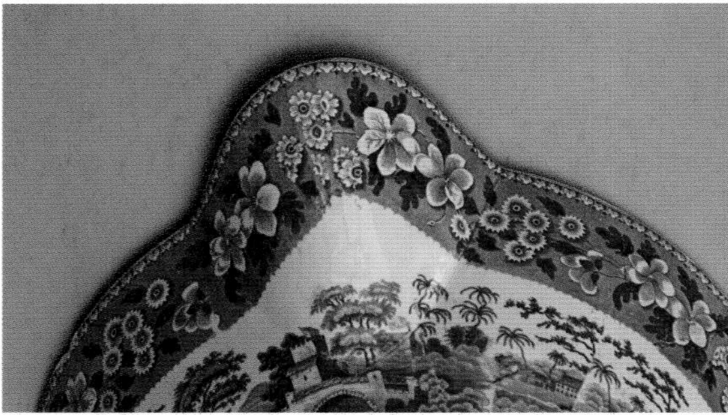

**Description:** A Spode large size "Tower" pattern skimming bowl, c.1820. This design was taken from a published work *Views of Rome and its Vicinity, J. Merigot and R. Edwards, 1796-98* and is entitled "Ponte Salaro." This bowl was used in a dairy environment for milk products such as cheese, cream, butter, and milk. The raw dairy product would be placed in this bowl and the cream that floated to the top would be skimmed off to use as cream or in butter production. The remaining milk would then be poured out using the beak and sieved. This ingenious, but highly important bowl is uncommon. It was used in conjunction with the Spode "Tower" pattern milk sieving device, which follows.
**Size:** 18.75" (47.5cm) wide including spout, 5.75" (14.5cm) deep.
**Marks:** Blue printed Spode.

# SPODE TOWER PATTERN MILK SIEVE

**Description:** A Spode "Tower" pattern bowl designed to be used in the refining process of milk, c.1820. This print was taken from a published work *Views of Rome and its Vicinity, J. Merigot and R. Edwards, 1796-98* and is entitled "Ponte Salaro." This intriguing object was to be used in conjunction with the skimming bowl (found at the start of this chapter). It has a flared and rounded rim (in place of a foot rim as in a normal bowl) where a piece of muslin would be tied. The bowl could then be used as a strainer or sieve. Note the manufacturer-made holes in the rim for hanging. Once the cream had been removed from the raw dairy product using the skimming bowl, the remaining contents would be carefully sieved through this bowl. Milk and dairy products were as important then as they are today.

**Size:** 6.25" (16cm) diameter, 3.5" (9cm) deep.

**Marks:** Blue printed SPODE.

# Spode Filigree Pattern Cress Drainer

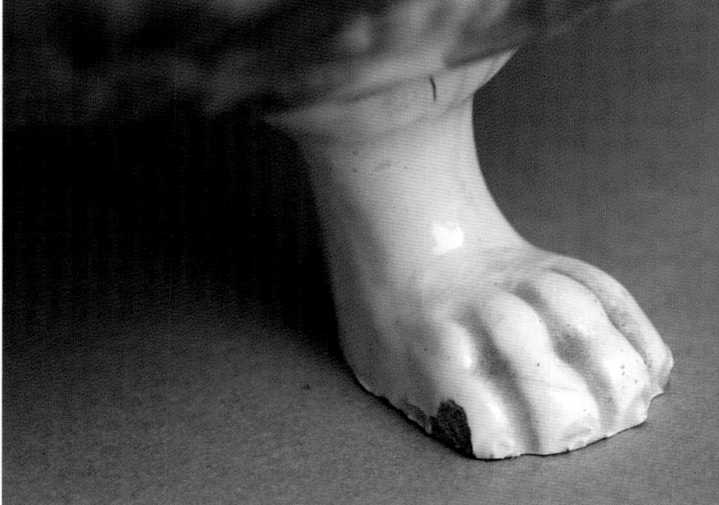

**Description:** A very unusual Spode "Filigree" pattern cress draining dish, c.1825. It is printed with a floral pattern that has a basket of mixed flowers to the centre and alternating vignettes of floral sprays and baskets of flowers around the border. This dish stands on three beautifully detailed lion's paw feet and probably would have had its own draining receptacle. This would have been a dished saucer-like object that would allow the cress to stand until it was sufficiently drained for use. The cress drainer has expertly pierced holes to the dished centre in the form of half moons, hearts, and circles. Cress was added to soups, sandwiches, and salads for its tangy flavour and for its nutritional value.
**Size:** 7" (18cm) in diameter, 2.25" (6cm) tall.
**Marks:** Blue printed SPODE.

# Spode Italian Pattern Stilton Pan & Cover

**Description:** A "New Shape" Spode "Italian" pattern stilton pan and cover, c.1820, printed with a scene of a romantic Italian landscape that was taken from a painting by Claude Lorraine, c.1638. This is surely one of *the* most famous patterns in transferware. The pan has a domed, removable cover which allowed easy access to the cheese that was being stored. This shape of cheese pan that had a lid was the best way to store cheese as it kept it from dust, moisture, and flies. Note that it has a pair of handles on the lower section so that the pan as a whole could be picked up safely and moved around the kitchen. These cheese pans with rather heavy covers seem to be very prone to damage and, as such, it seems they don't survive too well.

**Size:** 7.5" (19cm) tall, 9.5" (25cm) wide including the handles.

**Marks:** Blue printed SPODE.

# Milkmaid Pattern Gooseberry Jar

**Description:** A "Milkmaid" pattern gooseberry jar, c.1835, printed with a scene of two milkmaids in a romantic European landscape. There are two cows and three sheep in the foreground. In the background there is a group of buildings that look very Swiss-like and there is a church behind a gate on the right-hand side. This vessel was used to store gooseberries after the harvest and is also known as a preserve jar. Note how the rim has a very pronounced and flared edge. This was to allow a piece of muslin to be securely tied to keep the preserved fruit fresh, clean, and ready for serving. Fruit, as with any produce of the time, was processed soon after harvest and jars such as this example were an integral part of that important process.

**Size:** 8.75" (22cm) tall, 5" (13cm) in diameter.

**Marks:** Printed title mark.

# Rogers Fallow Deer Food Moulds

**Description:** A very unusual set of three Rogers "Fallow Deer" pattern food moulds, c.1825, printed with a scene of two deer before a pair of country cottages in a landscape. The two deer were taken from *A General History of Quadrupeds, Thomas Bewick, 1790.* Note how the engraver has added spots to the standing deer which was actually a Red Deer as engraved by Bewick. The moulds would be used in the production of pâtés, jellies, and any other food that needed to be set. The beauty of these moulds is that when the food was set, the mould could simply be slid off, rather than having to extract the food item from the more usual ramekin dish or similar vessel. Not many survive due to their fragile nature and the fact that they were possibly put in an oven. Another possible reason for there not being many examples known is that they might not have been too good at their job. If a viscous content was used that needed to be set, you can imagine it running out of the bottom rather too easily.
**Size:** 6.25" (16cm) x 2.5" (6.5cm) and 4.5" (11.5cm) x 1.75" (4.5cm).
**Marks:** Unmarked.

# Spode Tower Wine Bin

**Description:** A Spode "Tower" wine bin, c.1820. This pattern was taken from a published work *Views of Rome and its Vicinity, J. Merigot and R. Edwards, 1796-98* and is entitled "Ponte Salaro." This shape is an extremely rare form. It is rather like a footbath, but is much narrower. It has moulded faux-coopered bands around the outside that are also found on footbaths. These suggest to the eye that it is made of wood and is held together with metal bands. The wine bin would have been filled with ice or chilled water and used to store and chill wines before they were required for serving. Wine was an important and widely taken drink at mealtimes, much as it is today.

**Size:** 16.5" (42cm) long, 10.75" (27.5cm) wide, 10" (25.5cm) tall.

**Marks:** Impressed SPODE and a crown.

# Rural Scene Spiked Pot

**Description:** A jar (lacking its cover) printed with a wrap-around rural scene. The pattern includes a ruined building, a castle on a hill, a figure outside a very distinctive house, and a family having a picnic on a river bank. It has over forty sharp, moulded spikes to the interior. This was almost certainly used to completely "mix" an egg prior to scrambling. However, one must ask how this object was thoroughly cleaned after use as those spikes are very sharp and access is minimal. It would have also taken some potting skill to make. All of those spikes would have been handmade and stuck into place which would have been incredibly difficult with the small amount of room available. They must also have been very prone to dropping off during the manufacturing process. Chickens were a widely kept livestock and egg dishes were extensively used in cooking during this period.

**Size:** 5.25" (13.5cm) tall, 4" (10cm) in diameter.

**Marks:** Unmarked.

# Minton Verona Pattern Flour Dredger

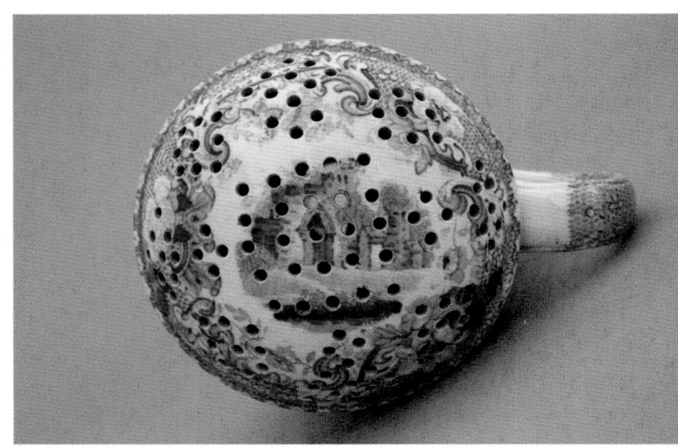

**Description:** A Minton "Verona" pattern flour dredger, c.1830, printed with a romantic Italianate landscape of cows before a ruin. It has a fixed top and the vessel was filled through a hole in the base. The hole was blocked by the use of a cork. This object was used to store flour and then to shake it out when required during a given cooking process. Although flour is the major ingredient in bread, it is also used in many other areas of cooking. This dredger was used most specifically in pastry making where it would be used to flour the board and rolling pin prior to the pastry being rolled. This prevented the pastry from sticking to either the rolling pin or board.

**Size:** 4.5" (11cm) wide, 5" (13cm) tall.

**Marks:** Blue printed Minton workman's mark.

# Wedgwood Rosewater Pourer

**Description:** A Wedgwood rosewater pourer, c.1815, printed with the famous "Long Bridge" pattern to both sides and has the border with no butterflies (moths). This shape of pot has a very interesting spout. It is shaped like a swan's neck, but the tip of the spout has three small holes. This could easily be confused with a suckling pot, but was actually for pouring rose water. Rose water is a by-product when making rose oil for use in perfume. It has a very distinctive flavour and is used as both a perfume and as a cooking flavour, but also as a component in some cosmetic and medical preparations and for religious purposes throughout Europe and Asia. This vessel would store and dispense the rose water when needed.

**Size:** 7" (18cm) long, 3.5" (9cm) tall.

**Marks:** Impressed WEDGWOOD.

# Enoch Wood Preserve Jar

**Description:** A preserve or gooseberry jar attributed to Enoch Wood, c.1825, with a wrap-around scene of a man shooting at snipe or woodcock; it is known as "Shooting with Dogs." This pattern is usually found printed only on hollowware items such as mugs and jugs. Maybe this is because the pattern, particularly being a wide scene, lends itself very well for this type of ware. The jar has a slightly flared rim so that a piece of muslin could be safely and securely tied to keep the contents in good order. In those days of pre-refrigeration, jars like this were extremely crucial. Fruit, as with any produce of the time, was processed soon after harvest and jars such as this example were an integral part of that important process.

**Size:** 9" (23cm) tall, 4.75" (12cm) in diameter.

**Marks:** Unmarked.

# Spode Lucano Bread Bin

**Description:** A Spode flat-lidded, circular bread bin, c.1820, well printed with the "Lucano" pattern. This was possibly taken from a source engraved by George Hackert entitled "The Tomb of Plautius Lucanus" and represents The Bridge of Lucano near Tivoli to the east of Rome. This large and impressive container was used much as we would use a bread bin today. It kept the bread in good condition for as long as possible. Objects such as these don't survive too well. It is very large and heavy, and the lid sits within a recess, so you can just imagine it being clanged on and off for nearly two hundred years. It really is a miracle that any of the utilitarian pieces survive.

**Size:** 14.5" (37cm) wide, 8" (20cm) tall.

**Marks:** Blue printed SPODE.

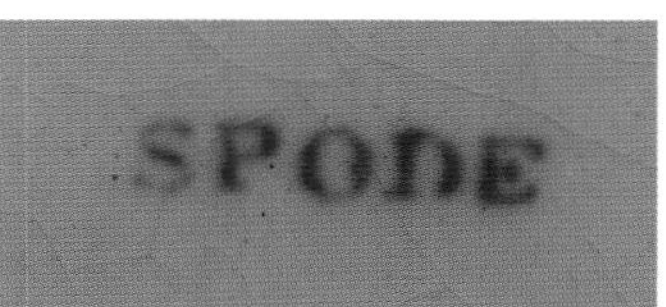

# Wedgwood Cress Dish

**Description:** A Wedgwood "Blue Rose" border series cress dish, c.1835, decorated with a scene of figures picnicking on a river bank before an ecclesiastical building within the famous "Blue Rose" border. This dish was used to drain cress or similar food stuffs prior to serving. It almost certainly had a draining dish in which it stood, that probably would also have been diamond-shaped and would have been dished and saucer-like. This would allow the cress to stand until it was sufficiently drained for use. Note the beautiful pierced shape of the draining holes and the four conical feet. Cress was added to soups, sandwiches, and salads for its tangy flavour and for its nutritional value.

**Size:** 7.25" (18.5cm) long.

**Marks:** Impressed WEDGWOOD.

# Spode Caramanian Stilton Pan & Cover

**Description:** A scarce Spode "Caramanian" stilton pan and cover, c.1810. Although this is a very handsome and majestic looking form, it was not too practical. The stilton wheel was difficult to access and cut once it was inside. This pan was quickly replaced with a "New Shape" that had a domed lid. Consequently, this makes this particular shape of pan a pretty rare object indeed. The base is printed with a scene of "Colossal Sarcophagus near Castle Rosso" to each side and the lid is printed with two scenes, "A Colossal Sarcophagus at Cacamo in Caramania" and "A Colossal Vase near Limisso in Cyprus." All three prints were taken from a published work entitled *Views in the Ottoman Empire* by Luigi Mayer, c.1803. Interestingly, the "Colossal Vase" is in the Louvre in Paris.

**Size:** 12.75" (32.5cm) wide, 7.5" (19cm) tall.

**Marks:** Blue printed Spode.

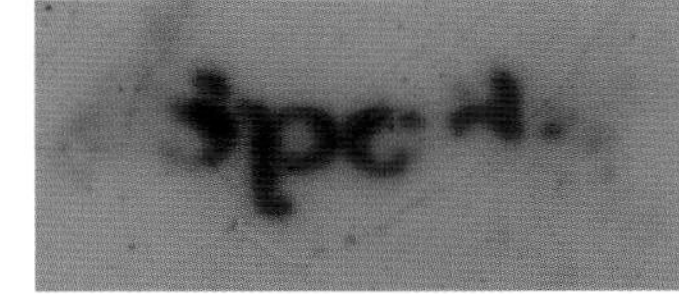

# Dry Mustard Pot & Cover

**Description:** A "Ladies with Parasol" pattern dry mustard pot and cover, c.1815, printed with a scene of two women holding a striped parasol. There is a very ornate fence behind them that leads to an unusual brick-built building. This chinoiserie patterned pot was used to store dry mustard before it was needed for use in cooking. Some dry mustard pots have screw tops, but this example does not. Mustard is a condiment that has been in popular use since the Roman period and is made from the seeds of various varieties of mustard plants. It is used in many areas and branches of cooking as a flavour or ingredient and is also an emulsifier that can stabilize a mixture of two or more un-blendable liquids such as oil and water.
**Size:** 4.25" (11cm) tall.
**Marks:** Unmarked.

# Two-handled Draining Dish

**Description:** A two-handled draining dish, c.1820. It is decorated with a wide floral border that includes passion flowers and has two cartouches to the exterior. One has a ruined abbey and the other has a man reading a book within a chinoiserie landscape. It has over ninety holes pierced into the dished, base area of the bowl. This dish was possibly a multi-purpose draining vessel such as a colander. It could be used to drain and strain a wide variety of food stuffs either over a bowl or in a sink. This vessel in transferware is extremely unusual and examples are few and far between.

**Size:** 6.5" (16.5cm) wide, 2.5" (6.5cm) tall.

**Marks:** Unmarked.

# Spode Parasol Figure Pudding Bowl

**Description:** A Spode "Parasol Figure" pattern pudding bowl, c.1825. The pattern on this bowl was a relatively late introduction to the Spode pattern range, especially in comparison to the other chinoiserie prints. It is an uncommon pattern, so obviously didn't sell too well as trends and fashions at this time had moved on. This bowl was used for steaming puddings such as sponge or plum puddings at Christmas time. Note how the rim is flared and shaped so that a piece of muslin could be placed over and tied on during the steaming process. As these bowls were being used often and in hot water during the steaming process, it stands to reason that not many survive.

**Size:** 6" (15cm) in diameter, 3.25" (8cm) tall.

**Marks:** Blue printed SPODE.

# Copeland & Garrett Storage Container

**Description:** A Copeland and Garrett storage container, c.1835, well printed with the "Castle" or "Gate of St. Sebastian at Capena" pattern. This scene was taken from a published work *Views of Rome and its Vicinity*, J. Merigot and R. Edwards, 1796-98. It has a moulded groove or recess 1" (2.5cm) down from the rim. This was to allow a piece of muslin to be securely tied and held in place. This vessel was very important in the days before refrigeration, when foods were processed, preserved, and stored at the time of harvest. Unusually, this vessel doesn't have handles. This may suggest that this item was not in frequent use or was used to store food stuffs for a longer period of time and remained in situ.
**Size:** 13.75" (35cm) long, 8" (20cm) deep, 12.5" (32cm) tall.
**Marks:** Indistinct printed C & G, Late Spode mark.

# Treacle Jar & Cover

**Description:** A screw top treacle jar and cover, c.1825, printed on both sides with a scene of two girls in a garden picking flowers. It has floral borders printed around the foot and rim. It has a moulded thread around the inner rim and lid which allowed the lid to be screwed securely into place. This type of vessel didn't survive very well because, if the lid was over tightened, it would cause cracking in the body, rendering the vessel useless. Treacle is a syrup made during the refining of sugar cane and is used chiefly in cooking as a form of sweetener or as a condiment. The screw top on this vessel would keep the syrup inside fresh and ready to use, and prevent sticky accidents.
**Size:** 5.75" (14.5cm) tall, 5.5" (14cm) wide.
**Marks:** Unmarked.

# A Florentine Pattern Veilleuse

**Description:** A "Florentine" pattern veilleuse or food warmer, c.1830, printed with a pattern that includes flowers and a snake wrapping around a vase. This pattern was made by several potters, but this example was probably made by Minton. A food warmer, as the name implies, was used to keep food warm, and was used mainly for invalids. The food was placed in the lidded bowl at the top and a reservoir of water sat below. In the base section, there would have been a heat source that would keep the water above warm, which in turn kept the food palatable. Note how the vessel at the top has a delicate pouring spout at the front and a lid to keep the warmth in.

**Size:** 9.75" (25cm) tall, 8.5" (21.5cm) tall.

**Marks:** Blue printed Florentine Stone China mark.

Chapter 2

# Dinner Ware

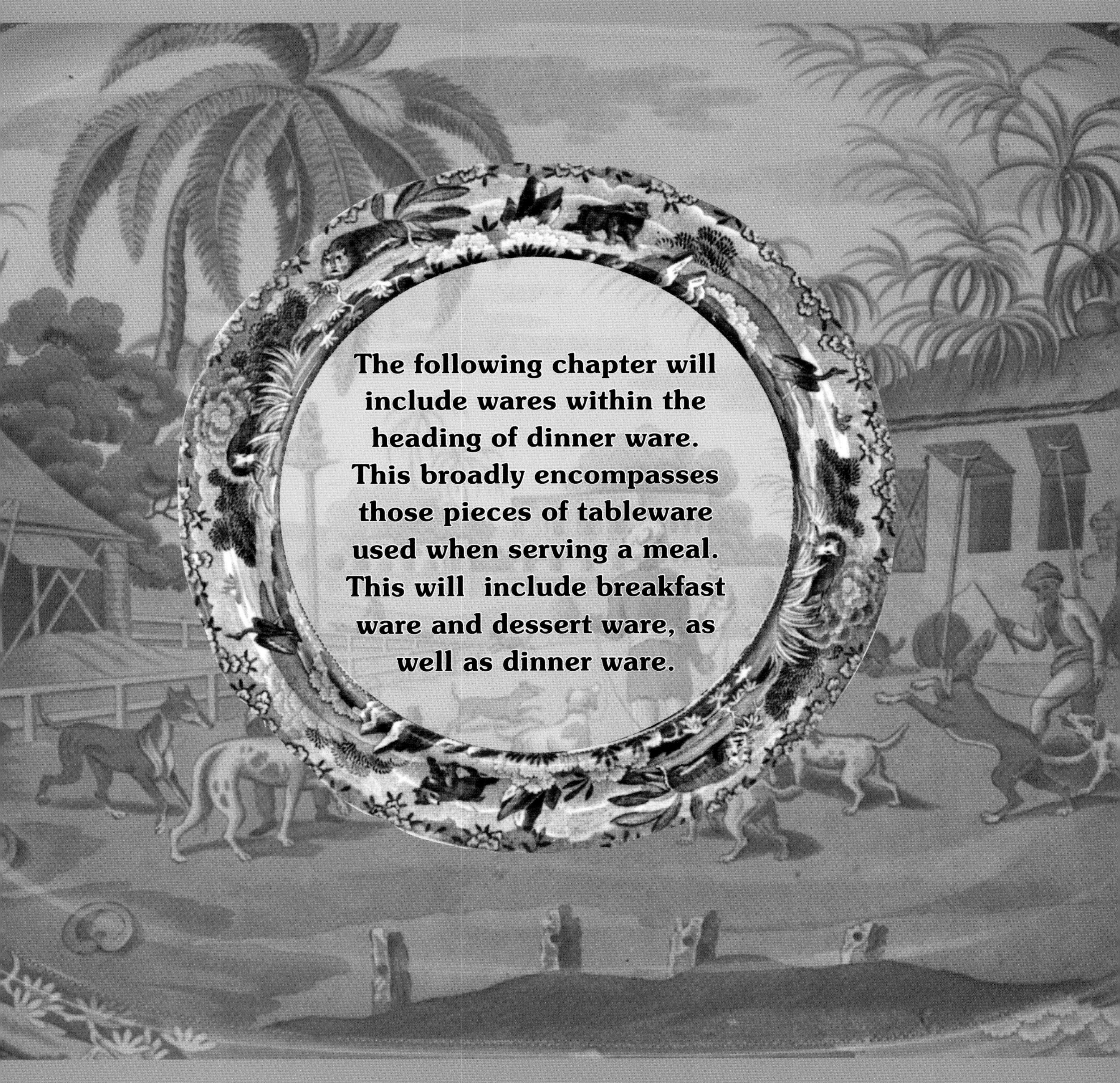

The following chapter will include wares within the heading of dinner ware. This broadly encompasses those pieces of tableware used when serving a meal. This will include breakfast ware and dessert ware, as well as dinner ware.

# Spode Caramanian Salmon Platter

**Description:** A simply stunning Spode "Caramanian" salmon platter, c.1810, printed with a view of " Triumphal Arch of Tripoli in Barbary." The Spode engravers used a source from a published work entitled *Views in the Ottoman Empire* by Luigi Mayer, c.1803. Note how the printer has had to use this single print twice in order to fill the sheer size of this dish. The potting is quite superb and the dish weighs an amazing 16lb (7.25Kg). It must have been almost impossible to manage when it had a fat salmon lying on it.

**Size:** 32" (81.5cm) long, 18.5" (47cm) tall.

**Marks:** Impressed SPODE and a crown.

# Carey Domestic Cattle Pickle Set

**Description:** A Thomas & John Carey "Domestic Cattle" complete pickle set, c.1820, printed with a scene of two cows, two sheep, a lamb, and a goat resting under a tree. The removable dishes are each printed with the same print of two cows wading in a stream. Pickle sets were for serving a wide variety of pickles, spices, and condiments during a meal. This series is attributed to Carey on the basis of marked examples being discovered, one of which is illustrated later in this chapter.
**Size:** 11.5" (29cm) long, dishes 5" (12.5cm) long.
**Marks:** Unmarked.

# Ship Carn Brea Castle Platter

**Description:** A beautiful well and tree platter, c.1825, printed with a maritime scene of a ship in full sail along a coastal scene. The platter has a blue printed title mark for "Ship Carn Brea Castle." A 19th century East India trading ship was named after Carn Brea Castle. This ship was wrecked off the Isle of Wight in 1829 and reported in *The Times* as being involved in excise tax fraud. It therefore stands to reason that the ship depicted on this platter is indeed *Carn Brea Castle*. Carn Brea Castle is a 14th century grade II listed granite building near Redruth, Cornwall. This platter has also been called "Falmouth Packet" in the past.

**Size:** 21" (53.5cm) wide.
**Marks:** Blue printed title mark.

# Brameld Asparagus Server

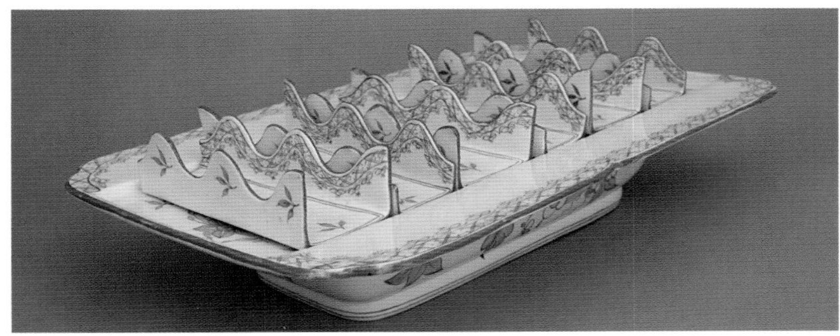

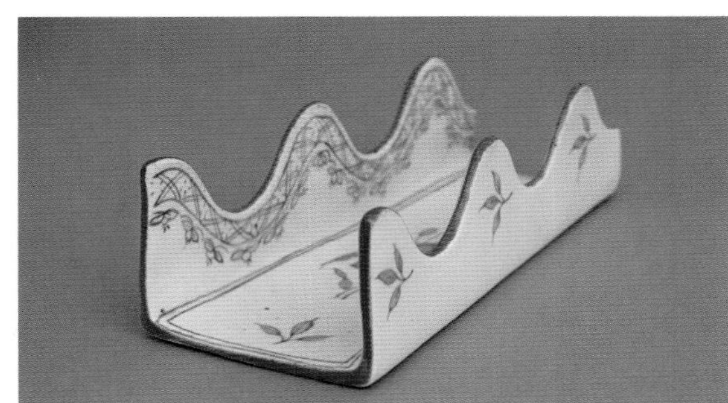

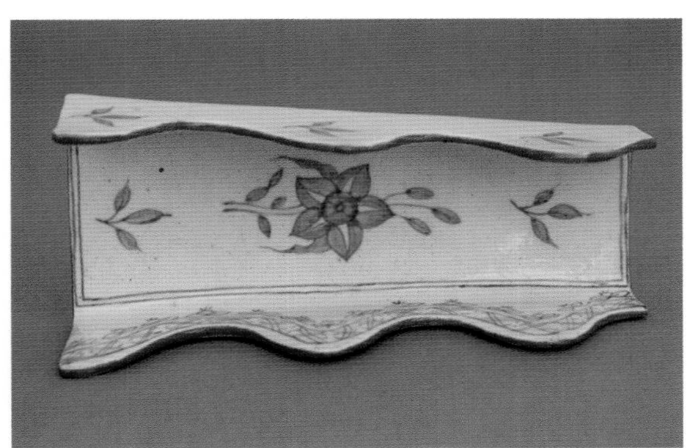

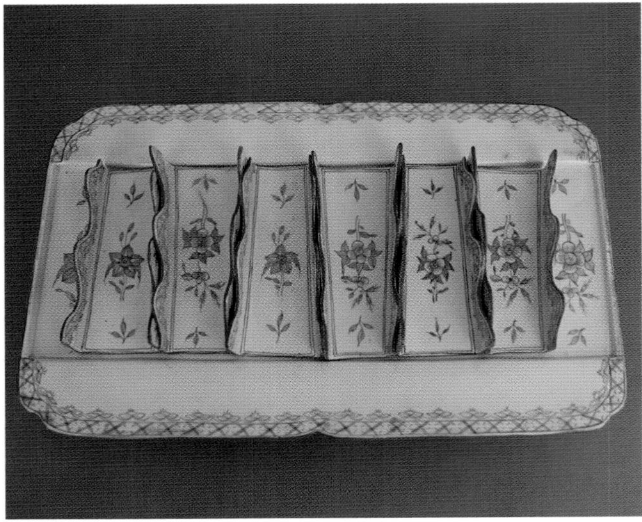

**Description:** A Brameld asparagus serving dish, c.1825, printed with a pattern known as "Stylised Flowers," with an ochre edge to all pieces. This ingenious serving device has a hot water reservoir above which sit six asparagus servers. This permitted the asparagus spears to remain warm until they were eaten. Asparagus servers are found from time to time, but to find a complete set such as this is a real treat and makes more sense of their intended use.
**Size:** 14.25" (36cm) x 8.75" (22cm) x 2.75" (7cm).
**Marks:** Impressed BRAMELD.

# Large Spode Caramanian Mug

**Description:** A Spode "Caramanian" series large mug, c.1810, printed with "Colossal Sarcophagus near Castle Rosso," which was taken from a published work entitled *Views in the Ottoman Empire* by Luigi Mayer, c.1803. Large mugs like this example were primarily used to serve ale, porter, and cider during the course of a meal. They are sometimes referred to as porter mugs. They seem to be quite prone to damage, probably because of the drink they contained, which meant that the user was a little less than careful after a few mugs full.

**Size:** 6" (15cm) tall.

**Marks:** Blue printed Spode.

# Carey Domestic Cattle Soup Ladle

**Description:** A Thomas & John Carey "Domestic Cattle" series soup ladle, c.1825, printed with a lovely scene of two dogs beneath a tree. It looks rather like one of the dogs is howling. The border is made up of flowers and bird's nests filled with eggs. This is a quite scarce series and soup ladles in themselves are uncommon survivors as it seems they were quite prone to damage.
**Size:** 12.5" (32cm) long.
**Marks:** Unmarked.

# Don Pottery Eyaopia Plate

**Description:** A Don Pottery plate, c.1820, printed with a scene of a white horse chasing a dog along a winding mountain road. This scene and border are taken from *Voyage pittoresque ou description des Royames de Naples et de Sicilie, Vol. IV,* c.1780, Saint Non, Jean Claude Richard. It shows a view of "Vue prise dans les environs de Leon forte." This is a village in central Sicily. The Don engraver added the white horse to the foreground. The border is made up of what appears to be heavily-adorned Grecian armour. There is a banner in the border that reads EYAOPIA. There was a slight error in the engraving of the word, but it is meant to translate as "Eulogy."

**Size:** 10" (25.5cm) in diameter.

**Marks:** Blue printed Don Pottery.

# Grazing Rabbits Pattern Egg Cup

**Description:** A "Grazing Rabbits" pattern egg cup, c.1815, printed with one of the rabbits and the farm house from the main pattern. Eggs cups are fairly scarce items, but especially so in this pattern. Egg cups were used to serve soft-boiled eggs, often with dippers, much as they are today. There were two forms of egg cups at this period: those that were made to go in a stand with others or in the centre of a supper set and those that were totally free-standing such as this pedestal example.
**Size:** 2.5" (6.5cm) tall.
**Marks:** Unmarked.

# Spode Oval Caramanian Supper Set

**Description:** A Spode "Caramanian" series oval supper set, c.1810, decorated with two different views. The outer dishes are printed with "Colossal Sarcophagus near Castle Rosso." The central tureen is printed with "Citadel near Corinth." They were taken from a published work entitled *Views in the Ottoman Empire* by Luigi Mayer, c.1803. It is complete with its contemporary mahogany tray with brass handles. The central tureen has a removable lid that reveals four removable egg cups and a salt. There is then a reservoir lining dish that would probably have held hot water to keep the eggs warm. Sets such as these were also used at breakfast time.

**Size:** 18.25" (46.5cm) in diameter.

**Marks:** Impressed Spode.

# SPODE CIRCULAR CARAMANIAN SUPPER SET

**Description:** A Spode "Caramanian" series circular supper set, c.1810, decorated with three different views. The outer dishes are printed with "Colossal Sarcophagus near Castle Rosso." The central circular base section and one side of the reversible cover have "Ancient Bath at Cacamo in Caramania." The other side of the cover has "Citadel near Corinth." They were taken from a published work entitled *Views in the Ottoman Empire* by Luigi Mayer, c.1803. It is complete with its contemporary mahogany tray with brass handles. Sets such as these were also used at breakfast time.
**Size:** 18.25" (46.5cm) in diameter.
**Marks:** Impressed SPODE.

# Willow Pattern Sauce Tureen

**Description:** A sauce tureen, c.1825, printed with the famous "Willow" pattern. The standard "Willow" pattern owes its design inspiration to the early Chinese wares. It is probably the most widely produced pattern in the history of transferware. The most amazing and unusual thing about this example is the handles. They are beautifully modelled as a standing bear to the lid and bear heads on the body of the tureen. This must surely be considered as being very rare.

**Size:** 7" (18cm) long, 4.5" (11.5cm) tall.

**Marks:** Unmarked.

# GAMEKEEPER BASKET & STAND

**Description:** A "Gamekeeper" pattern basket and stand, c.1820. This famous pattern of a game keeper and his dogs was taken from the published work *Rural Sports* by Rev. W. B. Daniel, 1812. The original print does not include the building in the central background. This is Goodwood House, Sussex, and was added to the design by the potter's engraver. The title mark is printed on a belt or possibly a dog collar. Basket and stands were primarily used for serving chestnuts, but also other fruit.

**Size:** 10.5" (27cm) wide.

**Marks:** Blue printed title mark.

# Spode Oyster Pan

**Description:** A Spode oyster pan, c.1820, printed with the "Lucano" pattern, which represents the Bridge of Lucano near Tivoli to the East of Rome. This design was possibly taken from an engraving by George Hackert entitled "The Tomb of Plautius Lucanus." An oyster pan was a two-handled vessel used to serve oysters. It was partly filled with ice and the oysters were placed on top to keep them fresh. It has faux moulded coopering to the sides that mimic wooden boards and coopered ribs. Only a handful of examples are known.

**Size:** 12.75" (32.5cm) x 10.75" (27cm) x 6" (15cm).

**Marks:** Spode workman's mark A.

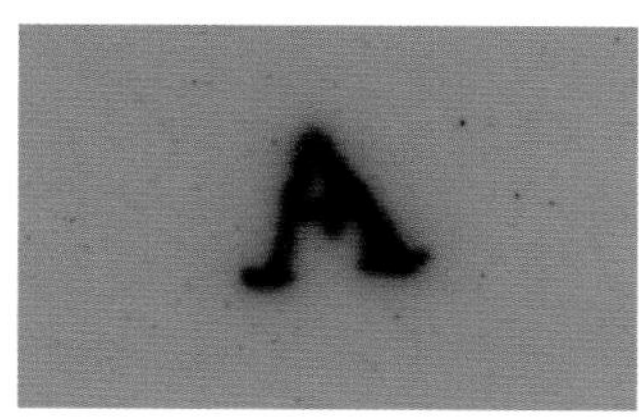

# Swansea Cheetah Plate

**Description:** A Swansea plate, c.1815, made by Dillwyn & Co. and beautifully printed with the "Cheetah" or "Leopard and Deer" pattern. The pattern was probably based on a print called "A Crouching Leopard Ready To Spring" from *A General History of Quadrupeds* by Thomas Bewick, 1790. This pattern is extremely rare.

**Size:** 9.75" (25cm) in diameter.

**Marks:** Unmarked.

# Pair of Spode Mustard Pots

**Description:** A pair of Spode mustard pots and covers, c.1820, both printed with a pattern called "Tiber," although the Spode factory name was "Rome." This pattern is made up of an out-of-place "Column of Trajan" and "Ponte St. Angelo" on the River Tiber which makes up the rest of the pattern. Both elements were taken from a published work *Views of Rome and its Vicinity* by J. Merigot and R. Edwards, 1796-98. These flat-lidded mustard pots have finely moulded ram's head handles and would be used to serve mustard at the dinner table.
**Size:** Each 2.5" (6.5cm) tall.
**Marks:** Blue printed SPODE.

# Condiment Spoon

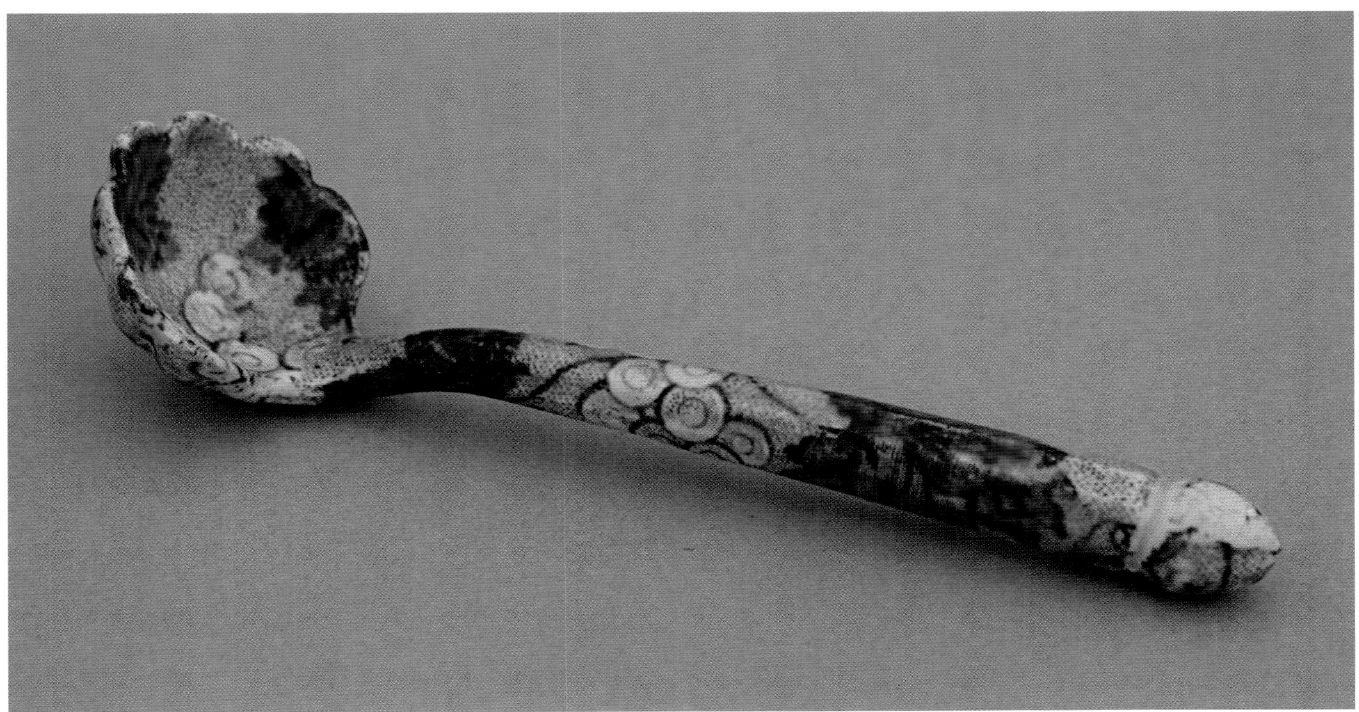

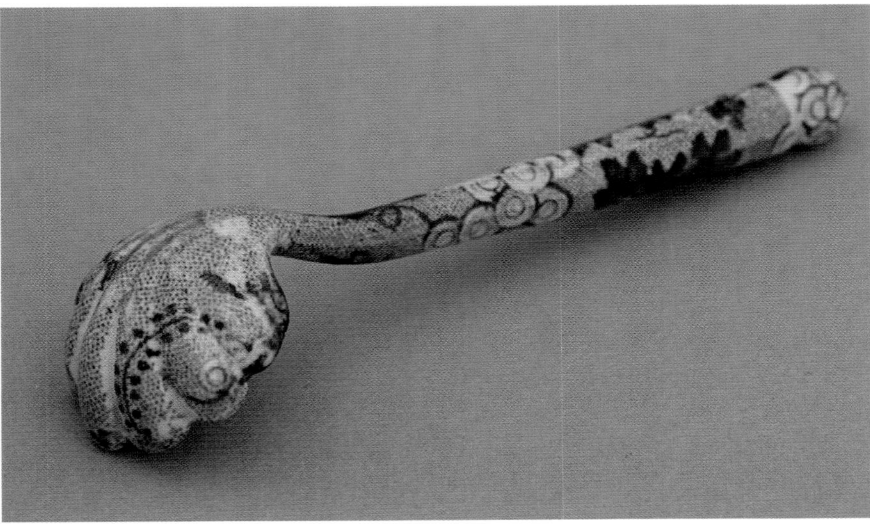

**Description:** A very unusual condiment spoon, c.1825. It is of moulded form with the bowl being of shell shape. It is a sheet pattern made up of grapes and grape vine. It was probably used to serve condiments or preserves on the dinner or breakfast table. Spoons like this are extremely rare as they were prone to damage and even being lost.
**Size:** 4" (10cm) long.
**Marks:** Unmarked.

# Spode Convolvulus Pattern Sauce Tureen

**Description:** A wonderful Spode "Convolvulus" or "Sunflower" pattern sauce tureen and cover, c.1820. This stunning pattern is made up largely of convolvulus and sunflowers. The pattern is uncommon and hollowware pieces such as this tureen are even more so. This shape of tureen is usually found printed with the "Caramanian" series.

**Size:** 6.25" (16cm) wide, 5.5" (14cm) tall.

**Marks:** Blue printed SPODE.

# Clews Castle Pattern Puzzle Jug

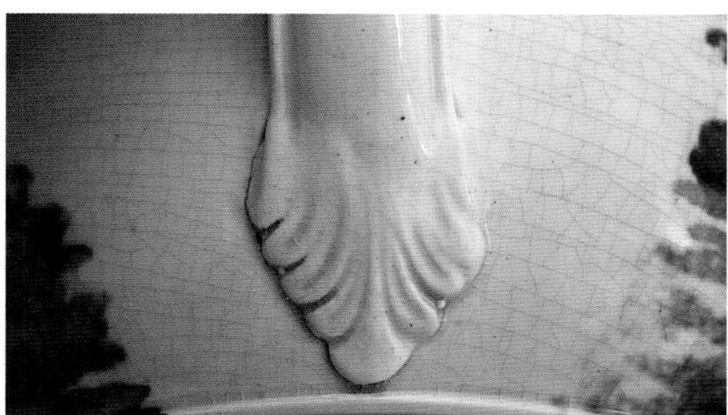

**Description:** A James & Ralph Clews puzzle jug, c.1825, well printed with the "Castle" or "Gate of St. Sebastian at Capena." This scene was taken from a published work *Views of Rome and its Vicinity*, by J. Merigot and R. Edwards, 1796-98. Unusually though, note how the pattern is printed in reverse or a mirror image of how it would normally appear. Puzzle jugs were an amusement of the time. The drinker would have to work out how to extract the liquid content without spilling any. This could only be achieved by covering two of the nozzles and a secret hole under the handle and sucking on the remaining spout.

**Size:** 8.25" (21cm) tall.

**Marks:** Blue printed Stone China mark.

# Spode Indian Sporting Soup Tureen & Cover

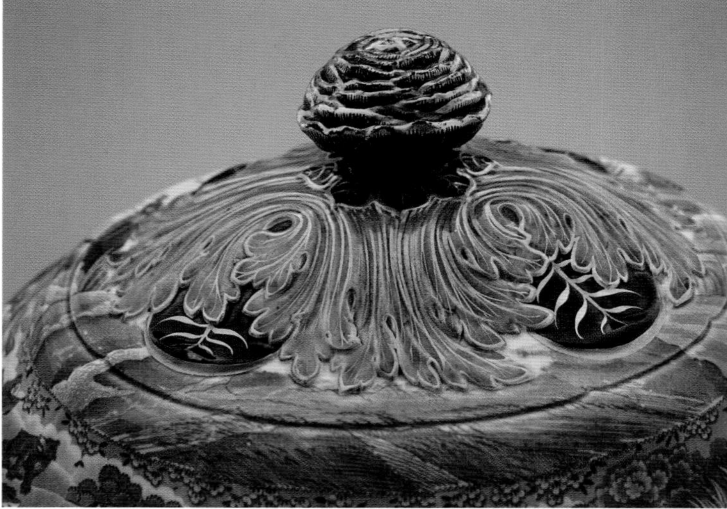

**Description:** A Spode "Indian Sporting" series soup tureen and cover, c.1810, printed with two scenes taken from a publication called *Oriental Field Sports* by T. Williamson, 1807. The lid is printed with "Hunting a Buffalo" and the body is printed with "The Hog at Bay" to both sides. This shape of tureen is very rare and only three or four examples are known. It has heavily moulded details to the body and lid. The lid has a huge acanthus leaf and rosebud finial while the tureen's handles are equally ornate. These features are picked out with gilding.

**Size:** 16.75" (42.5cm) wide, 12.75" (32.5cm) tall.

**Marks:** Blue printed SPODE and title marks.

THE HOG AT BAY

# Spode Argyle

**Description:** A Spode "Tower" pattern Argyle, c.1825. This was taken from a published work *Views of Rome and its Vicinity* by J. Merigot and R. Edwards, 1796-98, and is entitled "Ponte Salaro." An argyle is an ingenious vessel. It has a hot water reservoir in the lower section of the body. This would keep the gravy in the body of the vessel warm and stop globules of fat from forming. It is so called because it was invented in about 1750 by the Duke of Argyll who, frustrated by his gravy getting cold and fatty, designed this vessel to overcome the problem. Examples are rare.
**Size:** 7.25" (18.5cm) tall.
**Marks:** Blue printed SPODE.

# Rogers Ornithological Plate

**Description:** An arcaded plate, c.1825, made by John Rogers and Son and printed with a design of two birds in a landscape. This arcaded plate was part of a larger dessert service that would have been used to serve a wide variety of fruits and desserts after a main meal. This pattern appears to be unrecorded, but possibly consisted of a multiple of various scenes of birds, a different one on each of the pieces of the dessert service.

**Size:** 8.25" (21cm) in diameter.

**Marks:** Impressed ROGERS.

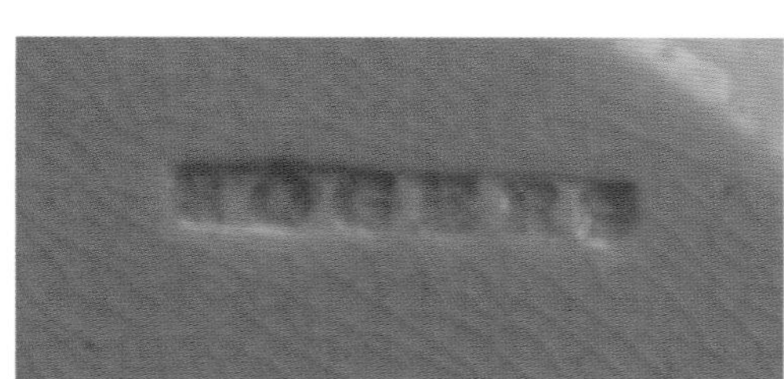

# Giant Knife Rest

**Description:** A large knife rest, c.1810, printed with a wide, geometric chinoiserie border print. It is a very unusual shape for a knife rest. They are usually flat, but this example is tall and triangular. Knife rests were used to rest the carving knife and fork on when not in use. They were supplied as a pair and are usually printed with just the border print that matches the rest of the service.

**Size:** 3.75" (9.5cm) long, 2.5" (6cm) tall.

**Marks:** Impressed LEEDS POTTERY.

# Good Ale Jug

**Description:** A blue printed jug with rural scenes, c.1825. This moulded jug is printed with two scenes. One depicts two men on horseback and their dogs stopping at an inn. The sign above the inn reads "Good," but other examples are known with the sign reading "Good Ale." A plough is also part of the inn's sign, so presumably, the inn was called "The Plough." The other side of the jug is printed with a fox hunting scene. Note the crisply moulded basket weave to the lower portion of the jug and the ornate handle.
**Size:** 6.25" (16cm) tall.
**Marks:** Unmarked.

# Spode Circular Well & Tree Platter

**Description:** A circular Spode well and tree platter, c.1825, well printed with the "Lucano" pattern. This was possibly taken from a source engraved by George Hackert entitled "The Tomb of Plautius Lucanus" and represents The Bridge of Lucano near Tivoli to the East of Rome. This large and unusually shaped platter is printed with two prints of the "Lucano" pattern. Note how the lower print is only partially printed. The platter could have been for serving really large cuts of meat or possibly large circular fish such as turbot. It could also possibly have been part of a set of graduated circular platters. If this is the case, their production was almost certainly short-lived as they were seen to take up too much room when not in use.

**Size:** 20.75" (53cm) in diameter.

**Marks:** Blue printed workman's mark A.

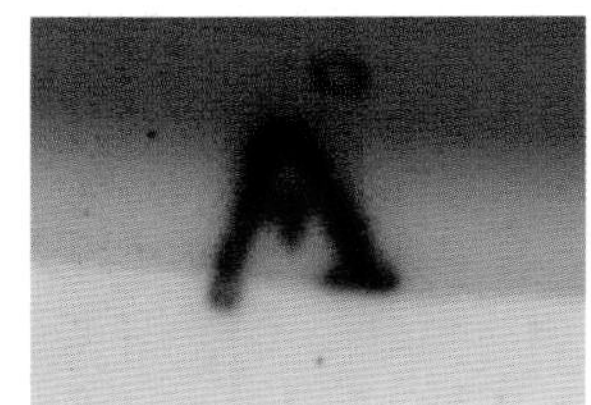

# Brameld Basket, Stand & Cover

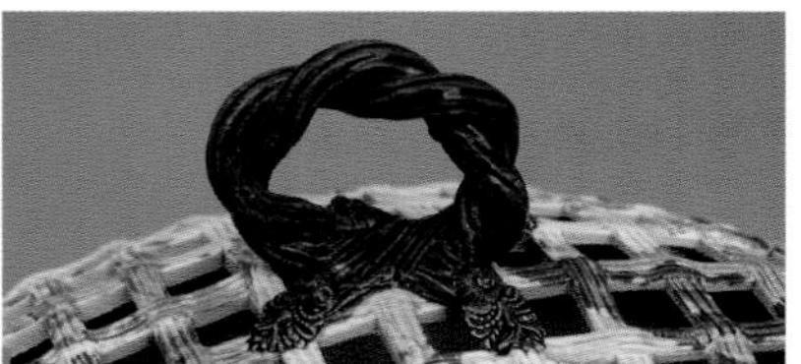

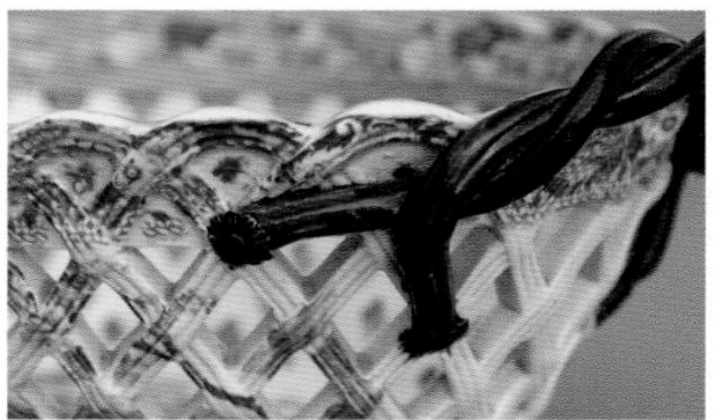

**Description:** A simply stunning Brameld basket, stand, and cover, c.1825, printed with the "Castle of Rochefort, South of France" pattern. Rochefort is a seaport on the Bay of Biscay at the mouth of the River Charente. Although the pattern title says "South of France," Rochefort is in the west of France. This wonderful piece is very unusual in that it has a lid. Baskets are very rarely found with lids. This example is of moulded basket weave form and has rope twist handles with floral embellishments. It is quite exquisite.

**Size:** 11" (28cm) wide, 8.25" (21cm) tall.

**Marks:** Impressed BRAMELD.

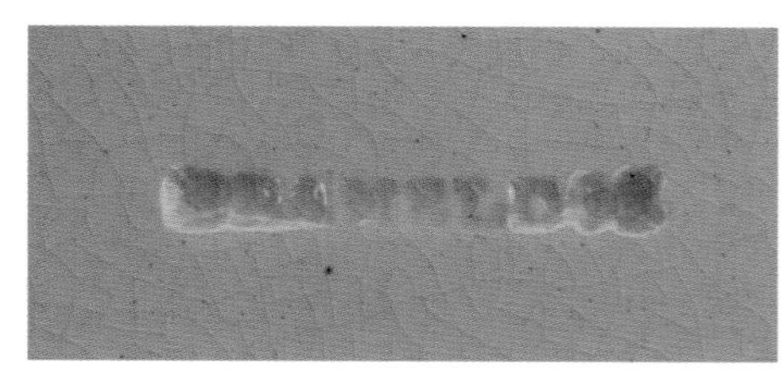

# Enormous Swansea Punch Bowl

**Description:** An incredible Swansea punch bowl, c.1810, printed to the centre with their famous "Swans" pattern. There are at least another fourteen different ornithological prints to the interior and exterior. These include a kingfisher, a cockerel, a peacock, a family of ducks, an eagle, and a family of pheasants. The source for the majority of these prints was a published work *The Ladies' Amusement, Sayer*, 1762. This type of bowl was used for serving punch, which was a very popular drink of the time. The word punch was taken from a Hindi word that described a drink made up of various constituent parts. The drink was brought back from India to England by sailors and employees of the East India Company in the early seventeenth century.

**Size:** 20.5" (52cm) in diameter.

**Marks:** Unmarked.

# Carey Domestic Cattle Plate

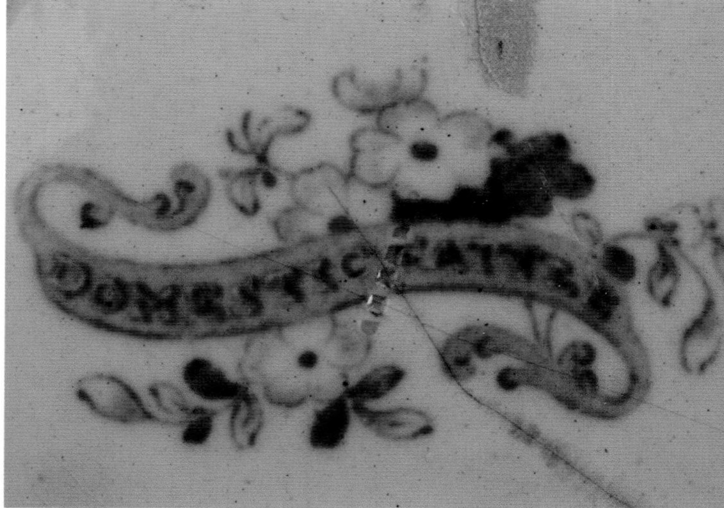

**Description:** A Thomas & John Carey "Domestic Cattle" series plate, c.1825, printed with a scene of three rabbits in a landscape. It has the usual series title mark of "DOMESTIC CATTLE" on the reverse. In addition, it also is impressed "CAREY' which is important and rare as this series is usually unmarked.

**Size:** 5.5" (14cm) in diameter.

**Marks:** Printed title mark, impressed CAREY.

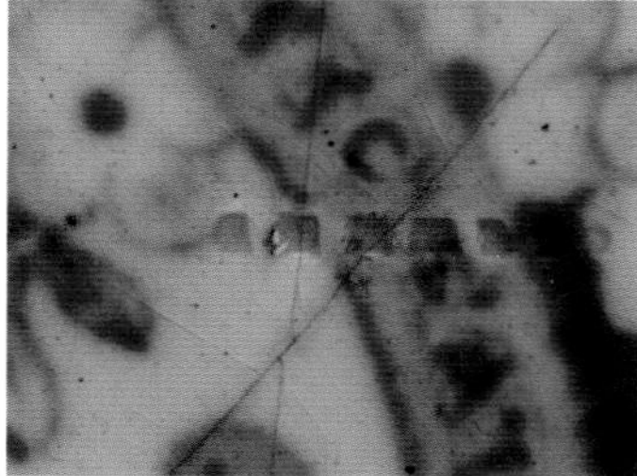

# Spode Indian Sporting Platter

**Description:** A Spode "Indian Sporting" series platter, c.1810, well printed with a titled scene of "Shooting A Leopard in a Tree." It shows a hunting scene in India in the late eighteenth/early nineteenth century. There are two men with rifles sitting on the backs of elephants. They are shooting at a leopard that has been cornered up a tree with the aid of a pack of dogs. This was during one of the great ages for exploration, hunting, shooting, and fishing. The source for this design was a publication called *Oriental Field Sports*, T. Williamson, 1807. This pattern also came on a well and tree platter. This series is one of the most prized and collected in transferware.

**Size:** 20.25" (51.5cm) wide.

**Marks:** Printed and impressed SPODE.

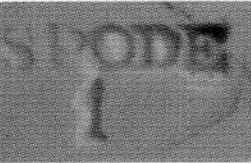

# Watson Jug

**Description:** A wonderful and amusing Watson and Company, Prestonpans, Scotland, jug, c.1815, printed with two amusing scenes that have rhymes above them. The first reads "Mouse…Let gang your gripes; fy, Madge! howt Baldy leers. / I wadne wish this had been seen. / 'Tis ease soft like___". The second reads; "Baldy And Yunder's Mouse: ay, ay, she hears far well. / When one like me comes rinning to the Bell / She and her cat sit beeking in her yard / To speak my errand, faith amaist by fear'd." They are written in a Scottish dialect, but the scenes printed below them do all the translating. Note the smiling faces of the bystanders as they watch the poor chap being beaten around the head with a brush!

**Size:** 7.75" (19.5cm) tall, 8.5" (21.5cm) handle to spout.

**Marks:** Blue printed WATSON & Co.

# Spode Caramanian Vinaigrette

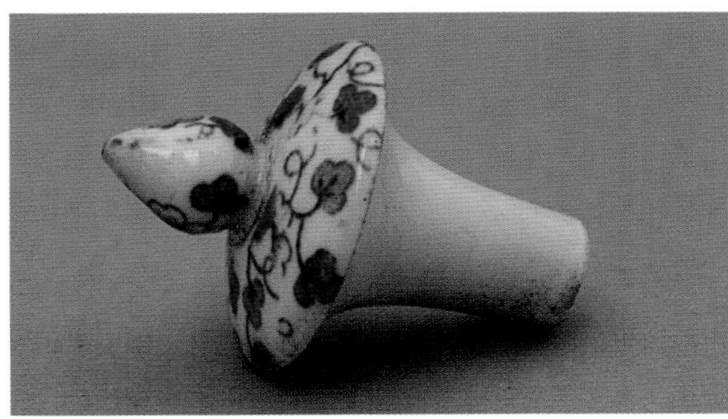

**Description:** A Spode "Caramanian" series vinaigrette, c.1810, printed with "Entrance to the Ancient Granary," which was taken from a published work entitled *Views in the Ottoman Empire* by Luigi Mayer, c.1803. It has a stopper that has a long stalk on it. This was either to help it remain securely in the vessel or was to aid the flow of the contents. How the stopper has stayed with this pot is a mystery as it is so small and delicate. This vessel was for serving vinegar or oil at the dinner table.

**Size:** 6" (15cm) tall.

**Marks:** Blue printed Spode.

# Vignette Series Supper Set Section

**Description:** A John Denton Bagster or (Baxter) "Vignette" series supper set dish, c.1825, printed with a charming rural scene from a series of many different rustic views. It has a dog running along with two horses and a group of people having a conversation. One person is holding a long rake. This dish is one of four dishes that would have made up the outer section of a supper set.
**Size:** 10.75" (27.5cm) long.
**Marks:** Unmarked.

# Spode Draining Ladle

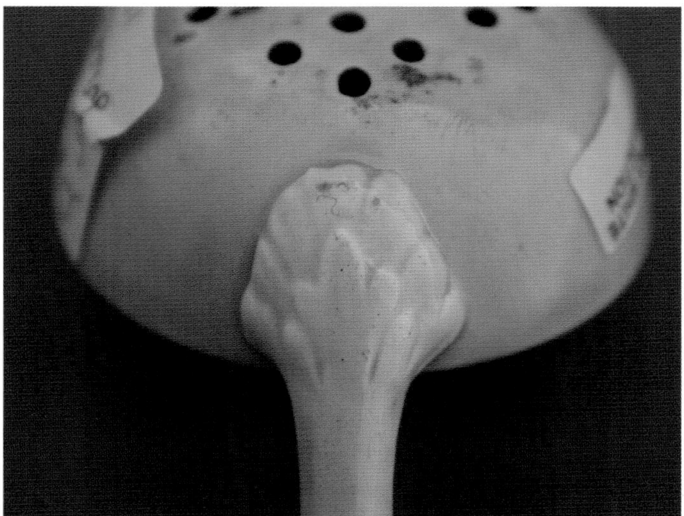

**Description:** A Spode "Forest Landscape" draining ladle, c.1815, printed with a chinoiserie scene of a forested foreground and buildings on an island in the middle of the pattern. The holes in the ladle were for draining small pieces of fruit prior to serving. It could also have been used for sifting sugar so was a multi-purpose item.
**Size:** 7" (18cm) long.
**Marks:** Unmarked.

# Greek Pattern Wine Cooler

**Description:** A stunning "Greek" pattern wine cooler, c.1815, printed with a wrap-around Grecian scene. It has previously been attributed to the Herculaneum factory. It is a high-quality piece and would have been partly filled with ice to chill a bottle of wine. Note the unusual handles and the very distinctive Greek key border.

**Size:** 9.25" (23.5cm) tall, 9" (23cm) wide.

**Marks:** Unmarked.

# Swansea Argyle

**Description:** A Swansea argyle, c.1800, printed with the "Fitzhugh" pattern. The pattern was copied from a Chinese service brought back by the Fitzhugh family, who were very active in the East India Trading company in the late 18th century. This, therefore, is where the pattern gets its name. An argyle is an ingenious vessel. It has a hot water reservoir in the body. This would keep the gravy in the body of the vessel warm and stop globules of fat from forming. It is so called as it was invented in about 1750 by the Duke of Argyll who, frustrated by his gravy getting cold and fatty, designed this vessel to overcome the problem. Examples are rare. Note how this example has a clever locking lid that sits on top of the hot water reservoir within the body of the vessel.
**Size:** 8" (20cm) tall, 7.5" (19cm) handle to spout.
**Marks:** Unmarked.

# Beemaster Pattern Soup Ladle

**Description:** A scarce "Beemaster" pattern soup ladle, c.1825. The pattern was taken from the painting *Swarm of Bees, Autumn* by George Robertson (1742-88). It shows a man carrying a bee skip and other figures before a country cottage. It has been suggested that the central man is blind and is being led by the boy. The border is made up of cartouches of animals that include deer, horses, and cows, and interspersed by flowers. Soup ladles are relatively uncommon as they were prone to being snapped and then discarded.
**Size:** 12.5" (32cm) long.
**Marks:** Unmarked.

# Flasher Pickle Dish

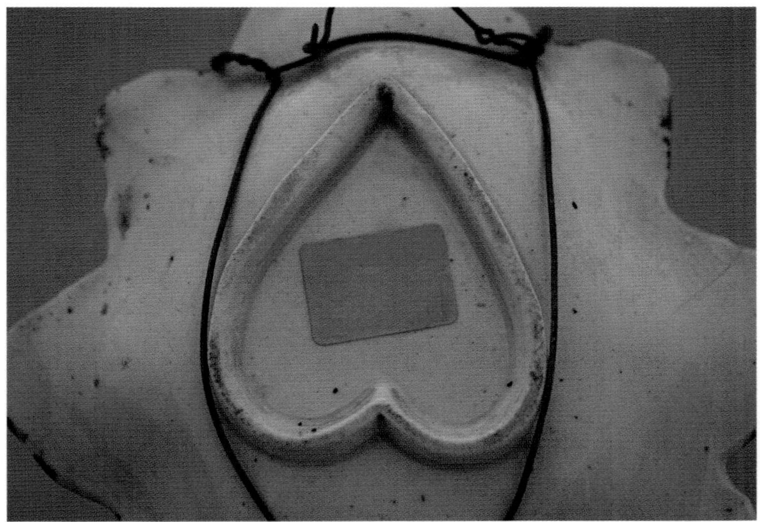

**Description:** An amusing "Flasher" pattern pickle dish, c.1820, printed with a scene of a woman and child and possibly a portly monk. It has been given the slightly unfortunate and amusing title. This is because it does look a little like the figure on the right is flashing. Note the very unusual heart-shaped foot rim. Pickle dishes were small, dished vessels that were used to serve a variety of food stuffs at a dinner table. They would hold spices, pickles, relishes and condiments.

**Size:** 6.5" (16.5cm) tall, 5.5" (14cm) wide.

**Marks:** Unmarked.

# Meir Flora Plate With Squirrel

**Description:** A John Meir "Flora" pattern plate, c.1825. Unusually for the "Flora" pattern, this example has the addition of a red squirrel on the left of the central vase of flowers. It was probably taken from a published work, *A Cabinet of Quadrupeds* by Church, 1805. This plate was almost certainly part of a full dinner service which would also have included the addition of the squirrel to the print. Maybe this variation was a special order service which would certainly back-up its rarity.

**Size:** 10" (25.5cm) in diameter.

**Marks:** Impressed crown.

# Rural Lidded Mustard Pot

**Description:** A mustard pot and cover, c.1825, printed with a charming rural scene of a man and a woman holding hands and skipping down a path towards a cottage. They are both holding long-handled rakes. It has a wide floral border. Note the aperture in the lid for a mustard spoon. Mustard is a condiment that has been in popular use since the Roman period and is made from the seeds of various varieties of mustard plant.
**Size:** 2.75" (7cm) tall.
**Marks:** Unmarked.

# Puzzle Jug

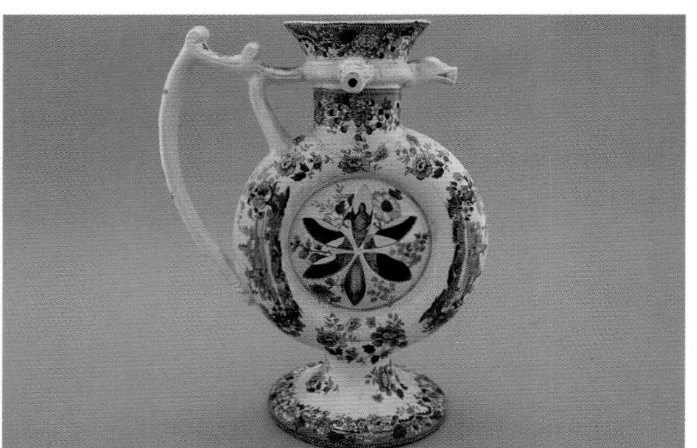

**Description:** A puzzle jug, c.1830, printed with a pattern very similar to "Pekin Sketches." It has a floral border and scenes of romantic Chinese landscapes. The spouts are moulded as griffin's heads and the tubes that connect them are moulded with scales. The most fascinating thing is the central wheel; within its centre there is a moulded figure. It is not quite clear enough to say if it's a Chinese man or maybe a woman, but it certainly is unusual.
**Size:** 11.25" (28.5cm) tall, 8.25" (21cm) wide.
**Marks:** Unmarked.

# Spode Claret Jug

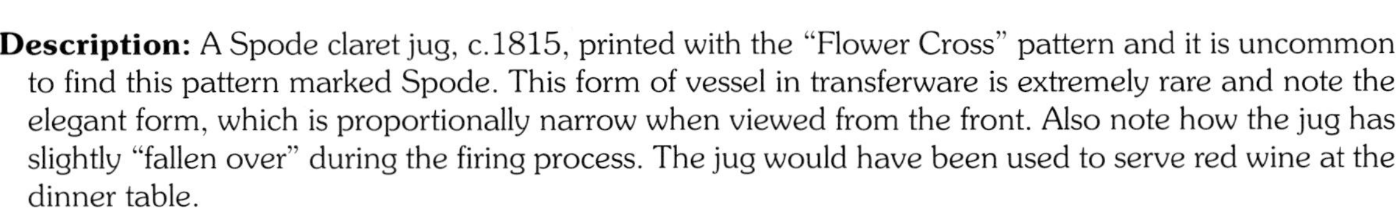

**Description:** A Spode claret jug, c.1815, printed with the "Flower Cross" pattern and it is uncommon to find this pattern marked Spode. This form of vessel in transferware is extremely rare and note the elegant form, which is proportionally narrow when viewed from the front. Also note how the jug has slightly "fallen over" during the firing process. The jug would have been used to serve red wine at the dinner table.

**Size:** 10.5" (27cm) tall.

**Marks:** Blue printed SPODE.

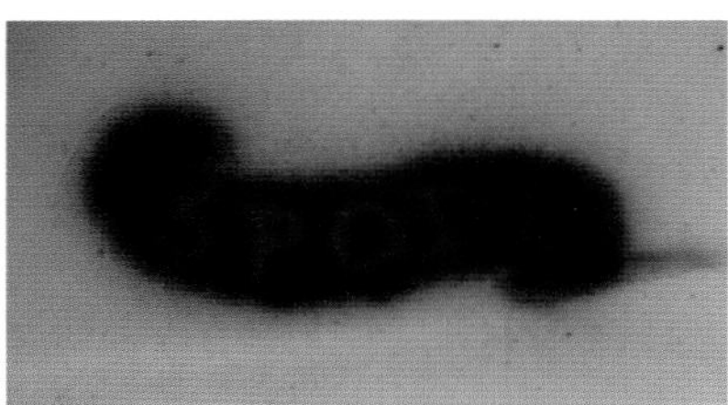

# Grazing Rabbits Jug

**Description:** A "Grazing Rabbits" pattern jug, c.1820, printed with a charming rural scene of three rabbits in a landscape. The most unusual aspect of this particular example is the use of the alternative borders. There is a wide floral border with long serrated leaves on the shoulder of the jug. There is then a different floral border with cartouches of chinoiserie scenes around the collar. Both of these patterns have been noted before on chinoiserie wares, but not in conjunction with each other.

**Size:** 8.5" (21.5cm) tall.

**Marks:** Unmarked.

# DURHAM OX JOHN DAY PLATTER

**Description:** A "Durham Ox" series platter, c.1810, printed with one of the most iconic prints in transferware, the "Durham Ox with John Day." The design was taken from an engraving by J. Whessell who in turn copied it from a painting by T. Boultbee, 1802. John Day, seen with the ox in this pattern, bought the ox for £250 in 1801. He toured England and Scotland with his ox in a specially designed cart for about six years, until the ox fell out of the cart and died. He was offered good money for the ox during his time as owner, but turned it all down. This proved to be a shrewd move as he made a fortune from his touring. The "Durham Ox" series has a wide and very distinctive stylised floral border.

**Size:** 21.75" (55cm) wide.

**Marks:** Unmarked.

# Durham Ox Quarry Platter

**Description:** A "Durham Ox" series platter, c.1810, printed with a scene called "The Quarry." The pattern is made up of four cows to the centre and a horse and cart to the left. On the right-hand side in the background, there are three men digging with pickaxes, which is where this particular scene gets its name. This series is generally quite scarce and much sought after. It consists of at least ten different rural views where livestock are the prominent theme.

**Size:** 18" (46cm) wide.

**Marks:** Unmarked.

# Spode Tower Giant Punch Pot

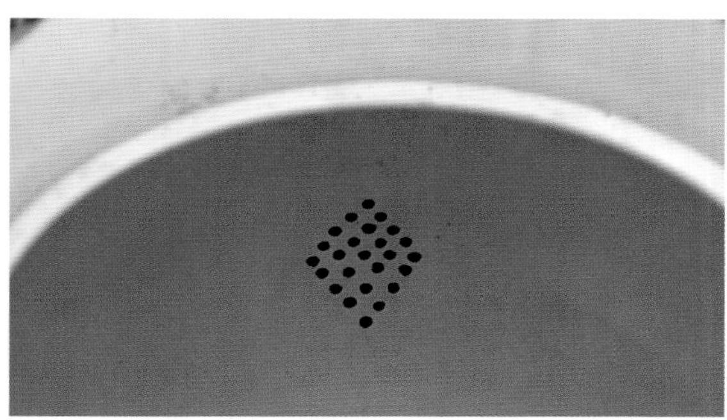

**Description:** A huge Spode "Tower" pattern punch pot and cover, c.1825. This design was taken from a published work *Views of Rome and its Vicinity* by J. Merigot and R. Edwards, 1796-98, and is entitled "Ponte Salaro." A punch pot was used for serving warm punch. Punch was a very popular drink of the time and the word punch was taken from a Hindi word that described a drink made up of various constituent parts. It might consist of sugar, lemon, tea, and alcohol. The image above also illustrates a Spode "Tower" child's teapot to give scale to the enormous punch pot.

**Size:** 11" (28cm) tall, 16.5" (42cm) handle to spout.

**Marks:** Blue printed SPODE.

# Spode Indian Sporting Pickle Set

**Description:** A Spode "Indian Sporting" series pickle set, c.1810. The diamond-shaped tray is printed with a titled scene of "Hunting a Hog Deer." This was taken from a publication called *Oriental Field Sports* by T. Williamson, 1807. Three of the central removable dishes are printed with sections from a print called "The Dead Hog," also from *Oriental Field Sports*. The remaining dish is printed with a section of border print. Pickle sets were for serving a wide variety of pickles, spices, and condiments during a meal.

**Size:** 11.25" (28.5cm) wide, dishes 5" (12.5cm) wide.

**Marks:** Blue printed SPODE & title mark.

# Don Pottery Sleeping Babe Plate

**Description:** A Don Pottery "Sleeping Babe" pattern plate, c.1825, printed with an all-over design of a child sleeping peacefully within a large group of flowers. The title of the plate reflects the subject very well. The engraving of this plate is exceptional and is of the highest quality. Note the unusual way that the central scene goes all the way to the edge of the plate and there is no border as such. This pattern is very rare and this example sits within a contemporary wooden frame that aids display.
**Size:** 10.5" (26cm) in diameter.
**Marks:** Blue printed DON POTTERY.

# SEA SHELL PLATE

**Description:** A very unusual shell-themed plate, c.1820, printed with an argonaut at the centre and eleven seashells around the border. An argonaut is part of a group of pelagic octopuses and are found in tropical and sub-tropical waters around the world. The border is also made up of seaweed. This plate was probably part of a bigger service and each item could have possibly been printed with different sea life.

**Size:** 6.25" (16cm) in diameter.

**Marks:** Unmarked.

# Spode Double-width Cheese Cradle

**Description:** A Spode cheese cradle, c.1820, printed with the "Castle" or "Gate of St. Sebastian at Capena" pattern. This scene was taken from a published work *Views of Rome and its Vicinity* by J. Merigot and R. Edwards, 1796-98. The really unusual and indeed rare thing about this example is its size or more specifically, its width. This cheese cradle is a double-width cradle which would be able to hold a wheel of stilton that was really huge.

**Size:** 12.25" (31cm) long, 8" (21cm) wide, 7.25" (18.5cm) tall.

**Marks:** Impressed and printed SPODE.

# Adams Lions Pattern Pickle Dishes

**Description:** A super pair of Adams "Lions" pattern pickle dishes, c.1820. They are each printed with the two separate elements from the main pattern. They are the "Lion" and the "Lioness and her cubs." The source for this design was *The Cyclopaedia of Arts, Sciences and Literature*, Longman, Hurst, Rees & Orme, 1807. Each dish is double printed with the same image, so they make a wonderful pair as they illustrate the pattern as a whole.
**Size:** Both 6.5" (16.5cm) tall, 6.25" (16cm) wide.
**Marks:** Unmarked.

# Palladian Porch Plate

**Description:** A very interesting "Palladian Porch" pattern plate, c.1833. As this pattern is not a known Spode design, there have been many theories about this plate. The most likely is that when Spode finished in 1833, the new owners, Copeland & Garrett, sold off the remaining undecorated high-quality blank Spode plates. Another potter bought this example and printed it with their own pattern. There was a lot of inter-trading among the potteries at this time. This pattern is made up of two prints taken from a published work entitled *Views in the Ottoman Empire* by Luigi Mayer, c.1803. The pillared building is from "Ancient Sepulchre near Macri" and the boat in the foreground comes from "Principal Entrance of the Harbour of Cacamo."

**Size:** 9.75" (25cm) in diameter.

**Marks:** Impressed Spode.

# Spode Fish Dish

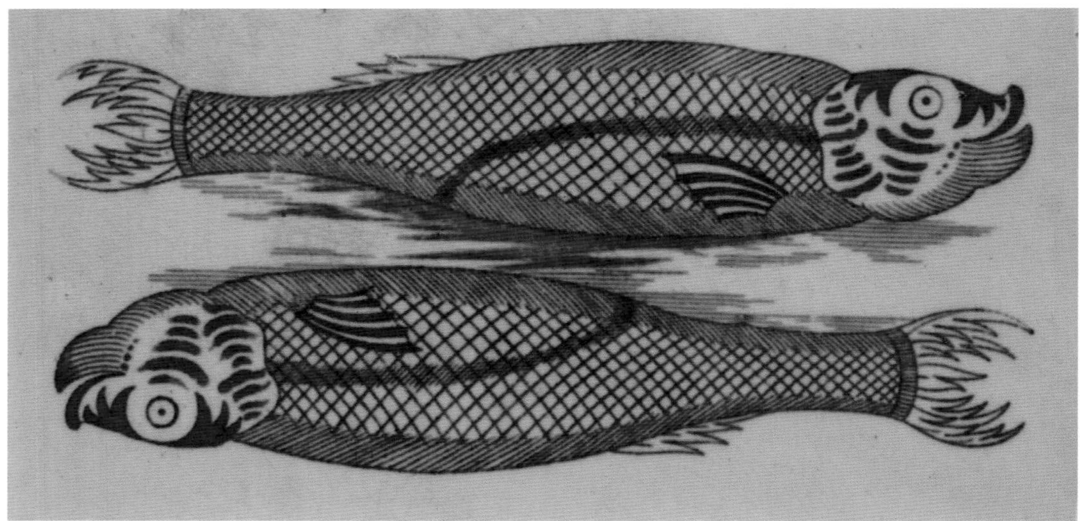

**Description:** An exquisite Spode dish, c.1815, printed with a "Willow" pattern border around the rim and a highlight colour to the edge of the rim known as "Foreign Edge." The centre is printed with two fish, which probably gives a clue as to the intended use of the dish. It might have been for serving smoked or potted fish, but must be considered to be an extreme rarity.

**Size:** 9.25" (23.5cm) wide.

**Marks:** Impressed SPODE.

# Brameld Pea Flower Vegetable Tureen

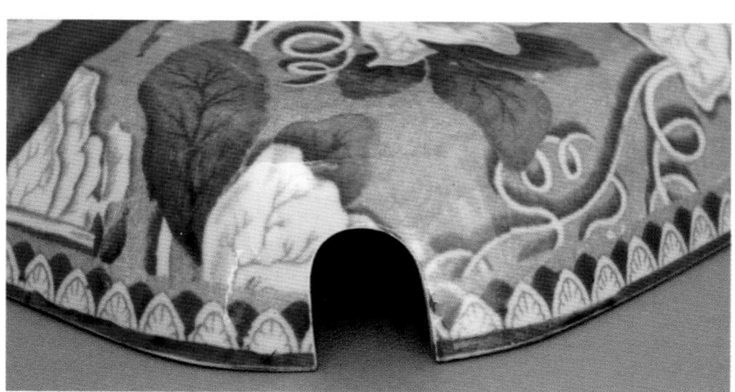

**Description:** A stunning Brameld "Pea Flower" pattern vegetable tureen and cover, c.1820, printed with this very famous sheet pattern that has pea plants with flowers and terminal tendrils. This pattern is often misnamed "Sweet Pea," but in the tea ware chapter you will find evidence that this is indeed a pea pattern and not sweet pea. The most unusual thing about this example is that it has a ladle aperture in the lid. Vegetable tureens almost never have this feature.

**Size:** 11" (28cm) wide, 5.75" (14.5cm) tall.

**Marks:** Impressed BRAMELD.

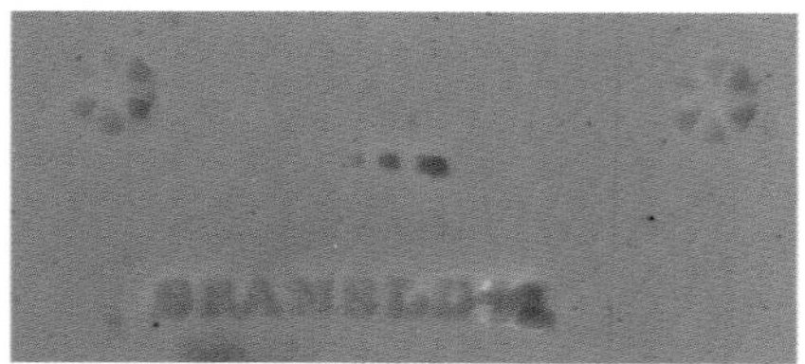

# Spode Star Flower Oyster Pan

**Description:** A Spode "Star Flower" pattern oyster pan, c. 1825, printed all over, both inside and out, with this very attractive Spode sheet pattern. It is very unusual for Spode to print the interior of a piece, but this pattern lends itself to this very well. It is also quite unusual to find this pattern without gilded or enamelled enhancements. An oyster pan would be partly filled with ice and then topped up with oysters. This would keep them cool and in good condition prior to serving.

**Size:** 16.5" (42cm) x 12" (30cm) x 6.25" (16cm).

**Marks:** Printed and impressed SPODE.

# ROGERS FALLOW DEER HORS-D'OEUVRE DISH

**Description:** A Rogers "Fallow Deer" pattern hors d'oeuvre dish, c.1825, printed with a scene of two deer before a country cottage in a landscape. The two deer were taken from *A General History of Quadrupeds* by Thomas Bewick, 1790. Note how the engraver has added spots to the standing deer which is actually a Red Deer as engraved by Bewick. This serving dish is rather similar to a pickle set, but it allowed larger quantities or even larger food stuffs to be served in the same way.

**Size:** 12.5" (32cm) handle to handle, dishes 10.5" (27cm) wide.

**Marks:** Impressed ROGERS.

# Durham Ox Series Dessert Comport

**Description:** A "Durham Ox" series dessert comport, c.1810, printed with two different scenes from the series. The interior is printed with a scene of a cowman with four cows and a calf. The exterior is printed with a scene of four cows and a bull in a landscape. Dinner wares in this series are scarce and dessert wares such as this example are even less common. Note how this piece has slightly collapsed in the firing process; from the side, you can see how misshapen it is.
**Size:** 13" (33cm) long, 4" (10cm) tall.
**Marks:** Unmarked.

# Spode Greek Pattern Ice Bucket

**Description:** A Spode "Greek" pattern giant pail-shaped ice bucket, c.1815. The Greek series is made up of three distinct elements: panel prints, centre prints, and vases. This bucket is printed with two vases (both the same) that were reserved for the larger pieces produced. The source for this was *Collection of Engravings from Ancient Vases of Greek Workmanship discovered in Sepulchres in the Kingdom of the Two Sicilies now in the Possession of William Hamilton* by W. Tischbein, c.1791. It is also printed with two identical panels of two women in Grecian dress. The source for this is not known. Ice pails were for storing ice at the table where it might be needed to top up an oyster pan, wine cooler, or similar vessel.

**Size:** 9.5" (24cm) tall, 8.25" (21cm) wide.

**Marks:** Indistinct workman's mark.

# Large Beemaster Jug

**Description:** A very impressive "Beemaster" pattern jug, c.1820, beautifully decorated with two prints of the famous and iconic "Beemaster" pattern. This design was taken from the painting *Swarm of Bees, Autumn* by George Robertson (1742-88). This huge jug possibly was for serving ale or cider, or may have even been a harvest jug. If so, it would have held cider for the farmers to drink when they were harvesting in the fields. Whatever its use, it is a really superb piece.

**Size:** 12.5" (32cm) tall, 13.75" (35cm) handle to spout.

**Marks:** Unmarked.

# Spode Broseley Pattern Guglet

**Description:** A Spode "Broseley" pattern footed guglet, c.1815, printed with a famous and widely produced design that was copied from a Chinese pattern. A guglet is a long-necked vessel used to store water before it is served at a dinner table. The name is of Anglo-Indian origin, but is also thought to be a description of the sound the water makes when it is poured, as it "glugs" out.
**Size:** 10.25" (26cm) tall.
**Marks:** Blue printed SPODE.

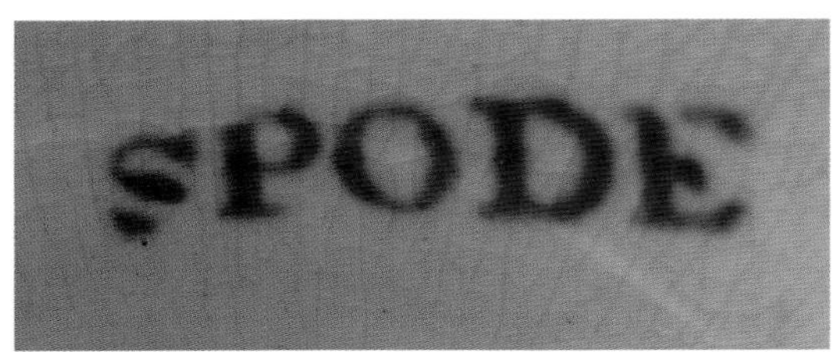

# ENOCH WOOD SPORTING SERIES LION PLATTER

**Description:** An Enoch Wood & Sons "Sporting Series" platter, c.1825, printed with a scene of a lion standing on a large rock looking over at a lioness and cub. The source for the lion on this platter was the frontispiece of *A Cabinet of Quadrupeds* by John Church, 1805. This, the largest platter from the service, is considered to be the rarest in the series. It was made for the large American export market of the time, but the colour of this example being slightly paler than usual does suggest that it was possibly intended for sale in the home market too.

**Size:** 20" (51cm) wide.

**Marks:** Impressed Enoch Wood & Sons.

# Enoch Wood Sporting Series Tiger Platter

**Description:** An Enoch Wood & Sons "Sporting Series" platter, c.1825, well printed with a scene of a tiger hunt, but the irony in the platter is clear to see; it's the tiger that is doing the hunting! The source for this pattern was *A Cabinet of Quadrupeds* by John Church, c.1805. This series was produced on dinner wares and toilet wares and was made for the large American export market of the time.

**Size:** 19" (48cm) wide.

**Marks:** Impressed Enoch Wood & Sons.

# Enoch Wood Sporting Series Polar Bear Platter

**Description:** An Enoch Wood & Sons "Sporting Series" platter, c.1825, printed with a scene of a polar bear and a family group of polar bears being attacked by hunters. There is a large sailing ship on the left-hand side of the print. The source for this pattern was *A Cabinet of Quadrupeds* by John Church, c.1805. This series was produced on dinner wares and toilet wares and was made for the large American export market of the time.

**Size:** 16.75" (42.5cm) wide.

**Marks:** Unmarked.

# Spode Caramanian Char Dish

**Description:** A Spode "Caramanian" series char dish, c.1810, printed with a pattern called "Ruins of an Ancient Temple near Corinth." This pattern is made up of two prints, "Ruins of an Ancient Temple near Corinth" and "A Caramanian family changing its abode." The source of these was a published work entitled *Views in the Ottoman Empire* by Luigi Mayer, c.1803. Char dishes in transferware are extremely rare with few examples known. They are much more usually seen in pearlware and creamware and are often decorated in pratt colours. A char dish was used to serve the fish char, which is a small trout-like fish of the genus *Salvelinus*.

**Size:** 10.75" (27.5cm) in diameter.

**Marks:** Printed and impressed SPODE.

# Wine Bottle Coaster

**Description:** A scarce wine bottle coaster, c.1825, printed with a pattern called "Gun Dogs," which shows a man shooting with a gun as his dogs accompany him. This pattern has been noted with an Enoch Wood & Sons impressed mark. Note the moulded handles. This vessel would have been used to hold a bottle on a dinner table. It would prevent any runs or drips of wine getting onto the table or tablecloth.

**Size:** 4.5" (11.5cm) tall, 5.75" (14.5cm) handle to handle.

**Marks:** Unmarked.

# Grazing Rabbits Tureen

**Description:** A "Grazing Rabbits" pattern tureen on fixed base and cover, c.1820, well printed with this much loved rural scene of three rabbits in a country scene. The fixed base of this vessel would ensure that the contents would not get onto the table or tablecloth if it ran down the body of the tureen. These vessels are often known as cream tureens. "Grazing Rabbits" is a fairly uncommon pattern these days and dessert wares are even more so. Note the delicate rope-twist handles.

**Size:** 8" (20cm) wide, 6.25" (16cm) tall.

**Marks:** Unmarked.

# Rural Scene Tankard

**Description:** A rural scene large tankard, c.1825, printed with an amusing wrap-around scene of an angry or escaping bull. There are two farmers in hot pursuit of the bull. They are being aided by two dogs, although it looks as if one dog is helping rather too much. You can see the rage of the bull, which is illustrated by the snorts emitting from his nose. This mug was used to serve ale, cider, or porter and can also be known as a porter mug.
**Size:** 5" (13cm) tall.
**Marks:** Unmarked.

# Brameld Shepherd Pattern Loving Cup

**Description:** A beautiful Brameld "Shepherd" pattern loving cup, c.1815. This very early pattern has a chinoiserie feel to it. It has a shepherd with a crook tending to his flock. His wife stands next to him holding a flower in her hand. There is a barn to the right-hand side of the pattern and cows on the hilly field in the background. A loving cup is a shared drinking vessel traditionally used at weddings and banquets and other similar celebratory occasions.

**Size:** 5.5" (14cm) tall, 7.5" (19cm) wide.

**Marks:** Blue printed workman's mark.

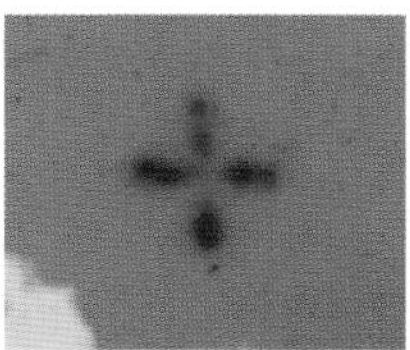

# Willow Pattern Wine Cooler

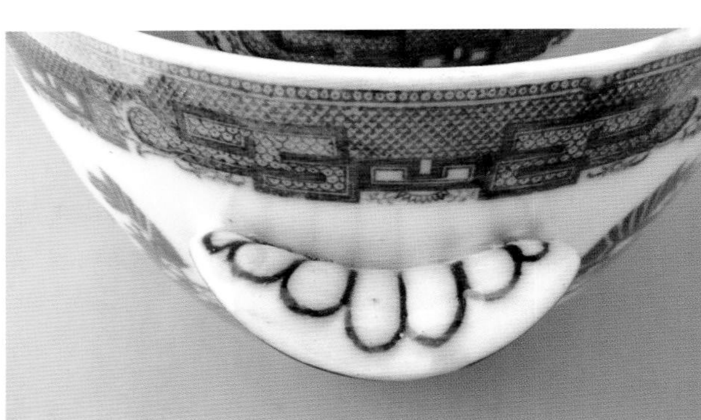

**Description:** A wine cooler, c.1815, printed in the standard "Willow" pattern. This form of wine cooler has a separate tube-like piece of pottery to the inside of the vessel. This was where the bottle sat. Ice was placed in the outer area to keep the wine chilled and at the desired temperature for serving. There were a couple of benefits from this design. Firstly, when the bottle was removed for pouring, the bottle wouldn't be dripping wet so that the table and table cloth wouldn't be in danger. Secondly, when the bottle was replaced in the cooler, you wouldn't have had to fight with the large amount of ice to get the bottle fully immersed. Note the very ornate and decorative handles.

**Size:** 7.5" (19cm) tall, 10" (25.5cm) handle to handle.

**Marks:** Indistinct workman's mark.

# WILD ROSE SHAPED TUREEN

**Description:** A very unusual "Wild Rose" tureen, stand, and cover, c.1825. It is well printed with a scene of "Nuneham Courtenay, Oxfordshire." It was taken from an engraving by W. Cooke, published 1 February 1811. The view depicts Nuneham Park House on the left, which was the seat of Earl Harcourt. The most distinctive and recognisable feature of the famous pattern is the arched bridge. This bridge was still in existence in living memory. The lock-keeper's cottage on the right of the pattern and the surrounding areas are said to have been part of a riverside walk designed by Capability Brown. The amazing tureen was probably a syllabub serving vessel. Note the very unusual, but elegant shape. Also note the fine moulding to the lid and the typical Georgian-style vase knop.

**Size:** 15" (38cm) tall, stand 11.5" (29cm) in diameter.

**Marks:** Unmarked.

# Brameld Pea Flower Tureen On Stand

**Description:** A stunning Brameld "Pea Flower" pattern supper set centre tureen on square stand, c.1820, well printed with Brameld's famous sheet pattern of pea flowers and tendrils. The tureen would have been part of a supper set and would have had dishes to go around the outside. It would have housed an egg stand, maybe egg cups, and a salt. The tureen has a very unusual separate square stand on which it sits. This would have raised the tureen up above the outer dishes.

**Size:** 12" (30cm) wide, 9.75" (25cm) tall.

**Marks:** Impressed BRAMELD.

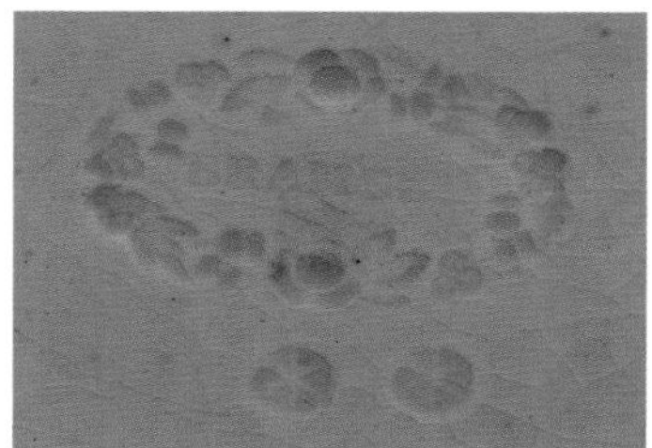

# Stevenson Springer Spaniel Soup Tureen

**Description:** A Ralph Stevenson Springer Spaniel soup tureen and cover, c.1825, printed with four panels, two each on the lid and body. They were taken from a published work *A Sportsman's Cabinet: Correct Delineation of the Various Dogs Used in the Sports of Field* by William Taplin, 1803. Note the elegant, scroll-form moulded handles that are printed with a sheet print.
**Size:** 15.75" (40cm) handle to handle, 11.5" (29cm) tall.
**Marks:** Unmarked.

Chapter 3

# Tea Ware

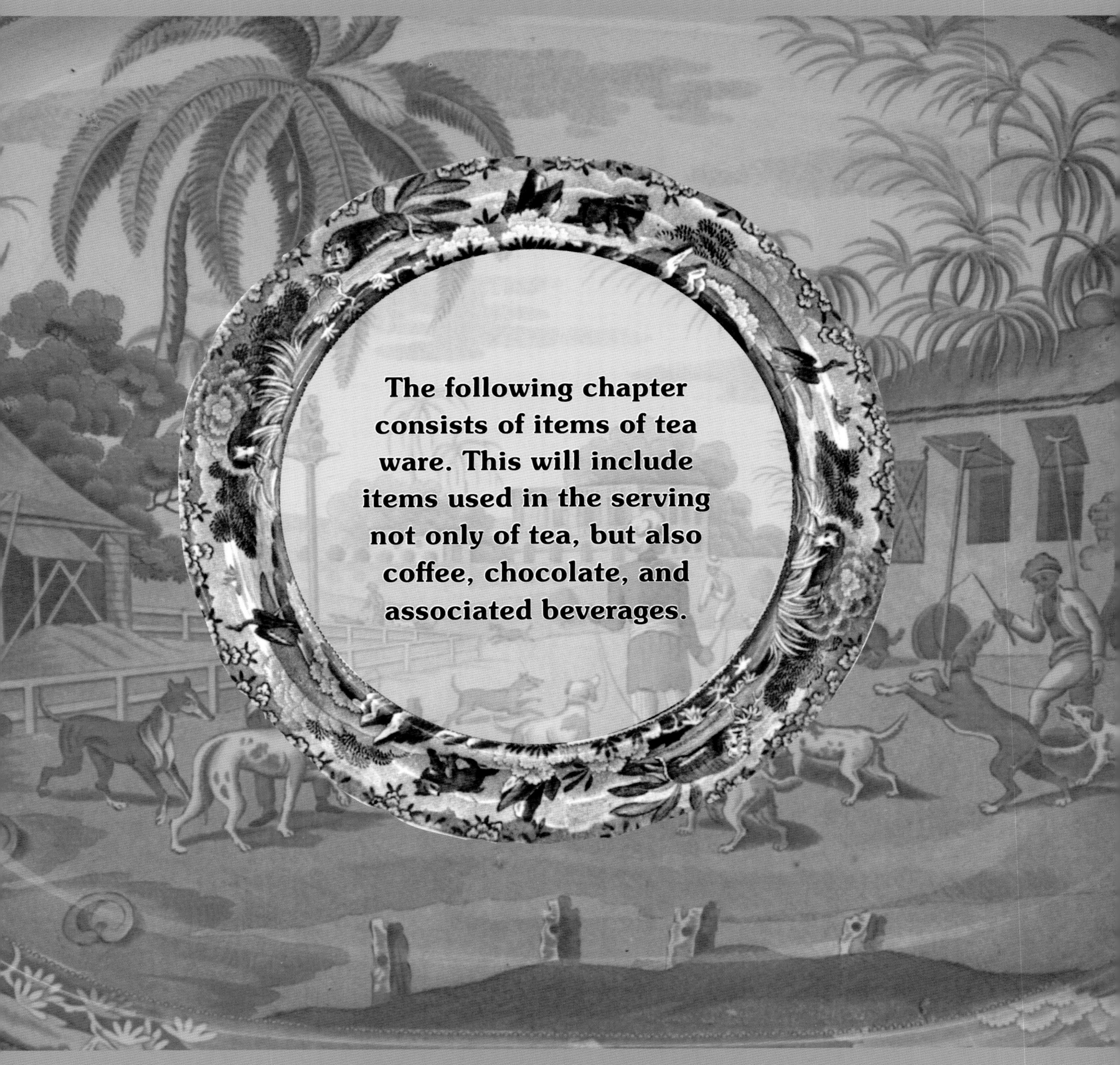

The following chapter consists of items of tea ware. This will include items used in the serving not only of tea, but also coffee, chocolate, and associated beverages.

# Cow Creamer

**Description:** A Cow Creamer, possibly Swansea, c.1820, printed with a scene of "Luscombe, Devon" in conjunction with a border from the "Blind Man's Buff" pattern. A cow creamer was a novelty vessel used to pour cream or milk when tea or coffee was being served. They are very prone to damage, especially to the cow's extremities and the lid was often dropped or lost. Blue printed cow creamers are scarce and tend to be found in the "Willow" pattern and date from at least 1840. This example is much earlier and is printed with a rural scene which makes it very special.
**Size:** 6.5" (16.5cm) long, 5.5" (14cm) tall.
**Marks:** Unmarked.

# Sawing Pattern Teapot

**Description:** A teapot, c.1825, well printed with a very unusual scene to both sides. It shows two men cutting up a tree with a two-man cross-cut saw. There is a ruined church in the background and a man walking a dog along a river bank. It is printed with a border of geometric lines and various floral sprays. Transferware sawing patterns are extremely rare and this might actually be unique. This teapot would have originally been part of a complete tea service that would have consisted of a set of tea bowls or cups and saucers, a sugar box, a waste bowl, and a creamer. There may also have been a teapot stand. Each piece may have been printed with this most unusual sawing scene, but also could quite easily have been printed with various other rural designs.
**Size:** 9.5" (24cm) long, 5.5" (14cm) tall.
**Marks:** Unmarked.

# Cottage Children Creamer

**Description:** A "Cottage Children" pattern cream jug, c.1820, printed with a scene of three children outside a cottage. They are looking at a pig poking his head out from his sty. Pigs on transferware must be considered to be uncommon and there are only a few patterns known to include them. Note how the smallest infant is climbing up the fence or gate to get a better look at the pig that has their attention. This jug would have been part of a tea or coffee service and would have held either milk or cream so that it could be added as necessary.

**Size:** 3.5" (9cm) tall.

**Marks:** Unmarked.

# Galloping Horse Hot Water Pot

**Description:** A hot water pot with locking cover, c.1810, well printed with the "Galloping Horse" pattern. This pattern, as the name suggests, has a somewhat energetic horse dashing through a chinoiserie landscape that includes pagodas, fences, and trees. A hot water pot was an essential part of a tea service and would hold hot water in reserve if it were needed to top up the teapot so that another cup or two could be extracted. As tea was so expensive, it was made to do as many cups as possible. This example has a very clever locking lid system so that the lid would not tip off when the pot was pouring.
**Size:** 5.25" (13.5cm) tall.
**Marks:** Unmarked.

# Milk & Honey Teabowl & Saucer

**Description:** A "Milk & Honey" teabowl and saucer, c.1825, printed with a scene of a beehive and a cow and calf outside a cottage. The border is made up of oak leaves and acorns. On the reverse, it has a blue printed title mark of "MILK & HONEY." Milk and honey were very important and widely used products at this time, much as they are today. The original expression, "a land flowing with milk and honey" is a biblical reference to the agricultural abundance of the Land of Israel. The first reference appears in the book of Exodus during Moses' vision of the burning bush.

**Size:** 4.75" (12cm) saucer diameter.

**Marks:** Printed title mark.

# Chocolate Pot With Pistol Grip Handle

**Description:** A chocolate pot, c.1830, printed with various floral designs and a wide border around the top and lid. The back of the pot is printed with a man on a horse in an Arabian landscape. This pot is a very unusual shape in that it has a pistol grip handle set at a right angle to the spout. Chocolate was a very popular and fashionable drink of the time and it was also very expensive. The Spanish brought cocoa beans back from the Mayans in the sixteenth century and over time it evolved and lost its original bitter taste by adding sugar and milk. The first chocolate house (similar to coffee houses) opened in 1657 and the craze spread from there. Chocolate was often the drink of choice of aristocratic ladies first thing in the morning, regularly served whilst they were still in bed.

**Size:** 6" (15cm) tall, 6" (15cm) wide including the handle.

**Marks:** Unmarked.

# Tea Canister

**Description:** An early chinoiserie tea canister and lid, c.1810, well printed with a pattern called "One Man on a Bridge" by an unknown maker. It has a wide and typically chinoiserie border that has moths or butterflies within it. Note how it has a long tube-like section below the rim of the lid that locates the lid within the body. This was to try and prevent the lid from tipping off and damaging both it and the delicate little finial on top. Tea canisters were an important part of tea drinking in the eighteenth and nineteenth centuries. They were used to store the very expensive and fashionable teas of the time. Note that it is a relatively small container; again, this reflects just how expensive a commodity tea was at this period.

**Size:** 5.75" (14.5cm) tall.

**Marks:** Blue printed workman's mark.

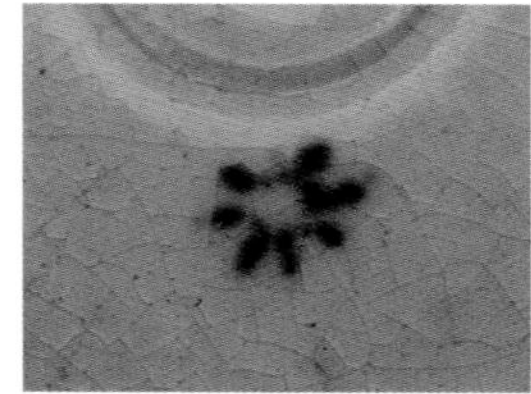

# Spode Temple Platter

**Description:** A very interesting bone china Spode "Temple" pattern platter, c.1815. On first examination, this platter looks like a trial piece where an apprentice printer has been learning his trade, but this is not the case. The actual truth is that someone ordered a "Temple" pattern tea service, but wanted a platter or tray with it. As "Temple" was only available on tea wares, the printer has taken a platter and printed it with parts of the tea ware pattern. Note how they have used the same section of the relatively small print many times to try to fill the expanse of the dish. The single boat at the top of the platter is a really lovely touch! There is another example of this later on in this chapter.

**Size:** 15.75" (40cm) long.

**Marks:** Blue printed SPODE.

# Swineherd Saucer

**Description:** A “Swineherd” pattern saucer, c.1825,well printed with a scene of a farmer and two pigs before a cottage. There is also a man carrying two pails of water. Pigs are rarely seen on transferware and there are only a few known patterns. It is not clear why this is the case, as pigs must have been quite a common animal during this time period. Pigs were raised as livestock by farmers for meat (pork, hams, gammon, or bacon), as well as for leather. Their bristly hairs were also used for brushes. Because of their excellent sense of smell, they are used to find truffles in many European countries. This saucer would have originally had either a tea bowl or a cup, and would have been part of a full tea or coffee service.
**Size:** 5.25” (13.5cm) in diameter.
**Marks:** Blue printed 5.

# Spode Blossom Plate

**Description:** A Spode "Blossom" small plate, c.1817, printed with a scene of a boy and a girl gathering water from a stream beneath a bridge. The border is made up of roses and rose leaves, grapes and grapevine, and a fruit that looks like a plum. The pattern name "Blossom" comes from a Spode factory proof book. This pattern is a very rare Spode print and marked examples are even less common. It has been noted on tea wares and breakfast wares. Its rarity nowadays maybe suggests that it had a short-lived production run, possibly due to a lack of popularity at the time. This seems quite hard to believe, as it is very charming and pleasing to the eye.

**Size:** 6.75" (17cm) in diameter.

**Marks:** Printed and impressed SPODE.

# Spode Honey Pot

**Description:** A Spode honey pot, c.1815, printed with the "Temple" pattern and has a fixed saucer-like base and a removable lid. Honey pots were an invaluable and carefully designed vessel used to store and serve honey at the tea table. The fixed saucer meant that any drips and runs from the pot would not go onto the table or table cloth. The main uses of honey are in cooking, baking, as a spread on bread, an addition to various beverages, such as tea, and a medical remedy. In the case of this vessel, the most likely use would have been at the tea or breakfast table, where honey was added to tea or used as a spread.

**Size:** 5" (13cm) wide, 4.5" (11.5cm) tall.

**Marks:** Blue printed Spode.

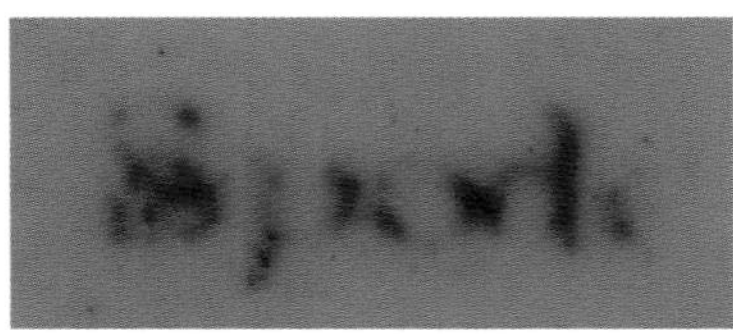

# Reindeer Cream Jug

**Description:** A very unusual Don Pottery "Reindeer" pattern pedestal cream jug, c.1820, printed with a curious scene of a woman milking a reindeer before a cottage. Two children look on. Reindeer milk has been drunk fresh or used to prepare cheese by the Sámi people in Finland for thousands of years. A traditional product is dried reindeer milk, which is prepared by softening it in coffee. Note how, on this particular example, the weight of the jug has caused the foot to slightly collapse during the manufacturing process. This is most obvious when viewed from the side as it takes on a slightly "drunken" look!

**Size:** 3.5" (9cm) in diameter.

**Marks:** Unmarked.

# FEEDING CHICKENS SAUCER

**Description:** A lovely "Feeding Chickens" saucer, c.1825, printed with a scene of a mother and child feeding their chickens and chicks. The most unusual part of the pattern is the border. Note the uncommon use of a basket weave which is very effective and realistic. Also note that the cottage has a name plaque above the door. This possibly reads "B W B." Was this to indicate the manufacturer or possibly the engraver was faithfully copying the source image? Maybe it was the engraver's initials? Chickens are one of the most common and widespread domestic animals and were kept primarily as a source of food for both their meat and their eggs.
**Size:** 5.25" (13.5cm) in diameter.
**Marks:** Unmarked.

# Two Teas Teapot

**Description:** A two teas teapot, c.1810, printed with the standard "Willow" pattern which is one of the most widely produced patterns within the whole field of transferware. This very ingenious pot is for serving two different teas from the same vessel. The basic principle is that it's a teapot within a teapot. When the main lid is removed, you will notice another lidded vessel inside. This kept the two tea flavours separate, but within the same container. The real trick was remembering which tea came out of which spout! This vessel is a real rarity and would have been for a high status person who could afford more than one variety of the expensive commodity, tea.
**Size:** 10" (25.5cm) tall, 14" (36cm) spout to spout.
**Marks:** Unmarked.

# Rural Scene Cup & Saucer

**Description:** A rural scene cup and saucer, c.1825. This lovely set is printed with a most unusual scene. It has a boy trying to scare crows away from his sheep. One of the crows is actually sitting on top of the sheep and protesting at the boy. It has a wide floral border with three cartouches that also contain flowers. Sheep were a very important livestock at this time, as they are today. They were kept to provide meat as well as wool and milk. They are a very popular subject in transferware, featuring in the background and foreground of many patterns. However, this pattern is a totally different take on the theme and just underlines how important sheep were to the people of the time. This is shown by the boy who is livid with the crow that seems to be annoying his precious livestock.

**Size:** Saucer 5.5" (14cm) in diameter.

**Marks:** Unmarked.

# Peace Pattern Chocolate Pot

**Description:** A "Peace" pattern chocolate pot and cover, c.1815, decorated with a scene that was probably meant to represent the end of the Napoleonic Wars and the long awaited peace. The pattern shows a figure that may be the Greek Goddess of Peace or, possibly, Britannia holding the Horn of Plenty. There are two messengers to the Gods holding scrolls that say "PEACE." Note that there is an owl on the spout of this pot. Owls are extremely rare birds on transferware and are a symbol of wisdom. This chocolate pot would have been part of a whole service that included cups and saucers, a sugar box, and a creamer. Chocolate was a very popular drink of this time amongst the upper and middle classes.
**Size:** 7.75" (19.5cm) tall.
**Marks:** Unmarked.

# SPODE CONTINENTAL PORT SAUCER

**Description:** An extremely rare and important Spode saucer, c.1825, printed with a pattern named "Continental Port." This saucer is one of only two known Spode examples of this pattern. There is a copper plate in the Spode works of this pattern and there is one known Copeland example, c.1908. The 1908 example was only printed at the factory out of curiosity to see what the pattern would have looked like. As such, it bears the Copeland mark from that period, but also the early SPODE mark that came off the copper plate. Until this saucer was found, it was not thought that any pieces were produced during the Spode period.

**Size:** 5.25" (13.5cm) in diameter.

**Marks:** Blue printed SPODE.

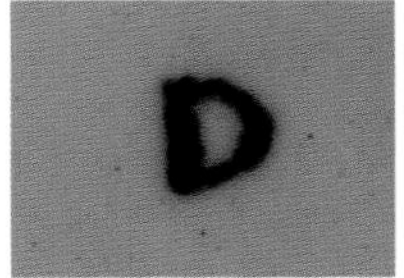

# Brameld Pea Flower Cup & Can

**Description:** A Brameld "Pea Flower" pattern cup and can, c.1820. These two items are printed with this beautiful floral design. However, the cup reveals something very interesting about the pattern. The interior is printed with a pea pod which shows that the pattern is actually made up of pea flowers and not sweet peas as is usually assumed. This pattern is quite uncommon on dinner ware, and is extremely rare on tea wares. These two pieces would have been from a much larger tea or coffee service that would have included a coffee pot/tea pot, a sugar box, a creamer, and a waste bowl.
**Size:** Both 2.5" (6.5cm) tall.
**Marks:** Unmarked.

# Bowling Tea Bowl & Saucer

**Description:** A most interesting tea bowl and saucer, c.1820, printed with a scene of bowling taking place before a country cottage. The origin of this game dates back many hundreds of years. It is difficult to determine if the pattern illustrates nine-pin bowling or skittles, as they were similar, but different, games. Nine pins at this time was played over a set distance and the object was to see who could knock down the pins in the least number of throws. Skittles involved both distance and "tipping" (short-distance throwing) and the winner would be the first to reach an agreed number of skittles knocked over. There were many regional variations, but what this pattern illustrates is a glimpse into the social and historical culture of the time.

**Size:** Saucer 5.5" (14cm) in diameter.

**Marks:** Unmarked.

# Two-handled Sugar Box

**Description:** A two-handled sucrier or sugar box, c.1825, printed with a very unusual scene of a lightning strike in a cloud-laden sky. There is what looks to be a scared young lady being consoled at the door by a man. This pattern has been tentatively attributed to Ridgway in the past. Note the two-handle form which is a more unusual, but elegant form of this vessel. Lightning is an atmospheric discharge of electricity accompanied by thunder, which typically occurs during thunderstorms. It is very unusual that inclement weather is depicted on works of art at this time, and especially not on transferware. The weather that is depicted in most transferware is idyllic, being sunny with scattered, fluffy clouds.
**Size:** 8" (20.5cm) wide, 5" (12.5cm) tall.
**Marks:** Unmarked.

# Brameld Conisbrough Castle Cup & Saucer, and Dished Plate

**Description:** A Brameld cup and saucer and dished plate, c.1825, all printed with a very interesting scene of "Conisbrough Castle." The castle was built during the 1180s by the fifth Earl of Surrey and is located in South Yorkshire near Mexborough. There are three key elements to the pattern, the castle, the River Don (note the partly sunken barge on the right), and the deer park. See how these three elements have been printed so differently among the pieces above.
**Size:** Saucer 4.75" (12cm) in diameter, dished plate 7.25" (18.5cm) diameter.
**Marks:** Unmarked.

# Tea Canister & Cover

**Description:** A tea canister and cover, c.1825, printed with a scene of two men in conversation outside a half-timbered building with a thatched roof. There is a sign hanging from the right-hand side of the building, which may suggest that it is a tavern or inn. Note how there is a long tube-like section below the rim of the lid that locates the lid within the body. This was to prevent the lid from tipping off and damaging both it and the delicate little finial on top. Tea canisters were used to store tea as part of a tea service. Note that this is a relatively small container; again, this reflects just how expensive tea was at this time. Canisters are, however, quite scarce, especially with their original lids.
**Size:** 5.5" (14cm) tall.
**Marks:** Unmarked.

# Rabbits Tea Plate

**Description:** A charming tea plate, c.1825, printed with a scene of three rabbits in a landscape. The pattern and border print have been noted on tea ware. This print is identical to that used by Thomas & John Carey on a "Domestic Cattle" plate seen in the dinner ware section of this book. Note how the potter has had to use the border print twice to fill the wide rim. Tea plates were part of a tea or coffee service that would have included a coffee pot/tea pot, a sugar box, a creamer, and a waste bowl. The tea plate would have been used to offer biscuits, small cakes and often thin slices of bread and butter when serving tea, coffee or chocolate. Occasions such as these were often social affairs.
**Size:** 8.5" (21.5cm) in diameter.
**Marks:** Unmarked.

# Saucer with Cat

**Description:** A blue printed saucer, c.1820, printed with a rural scene of a girl sitting with her cat on a bench outside a cottage. Cats are very rare creatures to find on transferware, especially at this time. There is a small blemish in the transfer on this example on the girl's mouth; it looks rather like she is smoking a cigarette! Cats have been associated with humans for at least 9,500 years and are currently the most popular pet in the world. Not only were they seen as pets at this time (which was a rare thing in itself), but they were also very useful for keeping mice and rats under control.
**Size:** 5.5" (14cm) in diameter.
**Marks:** Unmarked.

# Spode Tall Door Platter

**Description:** A Spode platter, c.1820, printed with the "Tall Door" pattern, which is so-called because the central doorway in the main building is proportionally very tall. The particularly unusual and interesting thing about this platter is that this pattern was only made on tea ware. Someone must have ordered a "Tall Door" pattern tea service, but wanted a platter or a tray with it. In order to accomplish this, the printer took the largest print available to him and printed it in the centre (you can clearly see the circular outline of this). Then, he filled the gaps on either side with two more prints. This was a clever solution to the problem. You can see another example of this technique earlier in this chapter.

**Size:** 14.75" (37.5cm) wide.

**Marks:** Impressed SPODE.

# Goat Milking Saucer

**Description:** A blue printed saucer, c.1825, printed with a scene of a goat being milked before a large church. A small girl is enjoying a sample tasting of the goat's milk. While goat milking is not that uncommon a practice, we are much more used to seeing cows being milked as a theme on transferware. A dairy goat in its prime produces an average of 6 to 8 pounds (2.7 to 3.6 kg) of milk daily. The milk is commonly processed into butter and cheese. Their milk is higher in protein, fat, and calories than cow's milk.

**Size:** 5.75" (14.5cm) in diameter.

**Marks:** Blue painted 10.

# Spode Love Chase Teapot

**Description:** A stunning Spode "Love Chase" pattern teapot, c.1815, printed with a scene from Greek mythology. It tells the story of Atalanta, Hippomenes, and the golden apples. In order to win the hand in marriage of Atalanta, Hippomenes distracted her with golden apples so he could beat her in a running race. It is very unusual to find this pattern without gilding to the rim and handle edges.
**Size:** 11" (28cm) long.
**Marks:** Unmarked.

# Cow Creamer

**Description:** A cow creamer, possibly Swansea, c.1820, printed with the "Squabbling Birds" pattern to both sides. This pattern shows two birds that really look like they are in heated conversation within a scene of mixed floral sprays and a long fence. A cow creamer was a novelty vessel used to pour cream or milk when tea or coffee was being served. They are very prone to damage, especially to the cow's extremities and the lid, which was often dropped or lost. Blue printed cow creamers are scarce and tend to be found in the "Willow" pattern and to date from at least 1840.
**Size:** 6.5" (16.5cm) long, 5.25" (13cm) tall.
**Marks:** Unmarked.

# Brameld Apple Gathers Saucer

**Description:** A lovely Brameld "Apple Gathers" saucer, c.1825, well printed with a charming and somewhat amusing rural scene. It depicts a family group picking apples from a large tree. The mother is standing at the foot of the tree catching the apples. The father is half way up the ladder picking from the lower branches, but it is the small boy who has been dispatched up the tree to pick those inaccessible apples! Apple trees were widely cultivated at this time and the crop was eaten or used in cooking. Cider production was also a huge business at this time and there were many different and regional ciders.

**Size:** 6.5" (16.5cm) in diameter.

**Marks:** Impressed BRAMELD.

# Tea Caddy Spoon

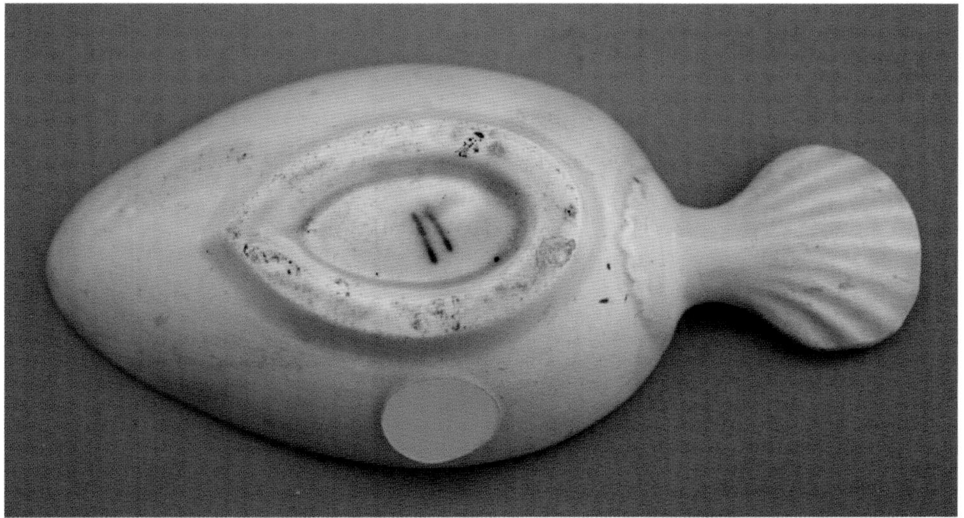

**Description:** A blue printed tea caddy spoon, c.1810, printed with a border and central print taken from a larger engraving. The border is similar to those used on the "Conversation" pattern, the "Two Figures II" pattern, as well as the "Full Nankin." The building at the centre is probably the island you see in the top centre of many chinoiserie patterns. Caddy spoons were used to extract and measure out tea from a caddy. This was at a time when tea was a very expensive commodity and none could afford to be wasted, hence the need to have a measuring tea caddy spoon. This form is also found in silver and porcelain, as well as other pottery bodies.

**Size:** 4" (10cm) long.

**Marks:** Two blue painted lines.

# Spode Country Scene Plate

**Description:** An extremely scarce Spode "Country Scene" plate, c.1820, printed with two cows in a wooded landscape before a ruin. The copper plate is still with the Spode Museum Trust and shards have been found at the Spode site, but almost no examples have been found. Even rarer is a marked example, which this plate is. It has only been noted on tea wares. Its rarity nowadays suggests that it had a short-lived production run, possibly due to a lack of popularity at the time. This seems quite hard to believe, as it is a lovely pattern.

**Size:** 7.25" (18.5cm) in diameter.

**Marks:** Impressed Spode.

# Minton Apple Tree Coffee Pot

**Description:** A lovely Minton "Apple Tree" pattern vase-shaped coffee pot, c.1820, printed with a scene of a man picking apples from a tree. He is throwing them down to a woman who appears to be catching them in her apron. Two children and a dog look on anxiously. This pattern is also known as "Picking Apples," but Minton's factory title was "Apple Tree." Note how the reverse side has a mirror transfer; this is most unusual. The pattern has a floral border that is found on the foot, the shoulder of the pot, and the rim of the lid. Note the typically Georgian style of the acorn finial on the lid.

**Size:** 10.5" (27cm) tall, 10" (25.5cm) handle to spout.

**Marks:** Blue printed workman's mark.

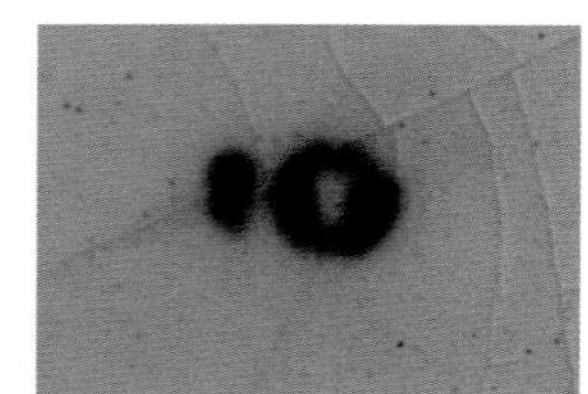

Chapter 4

# Toilet & Medical Ware

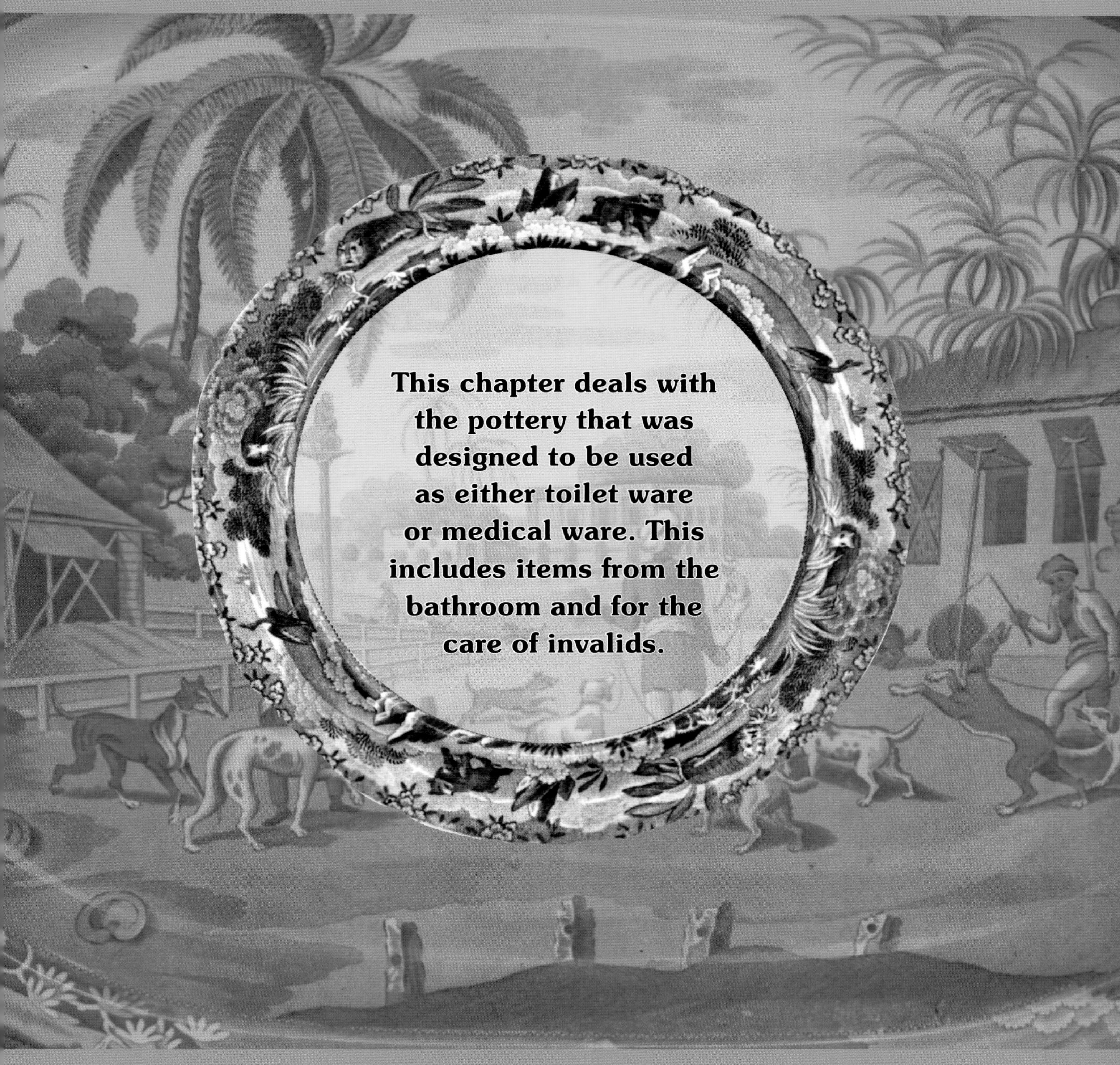

**This chapter deals with the pottery that was designed to be used as either toilet ware or medical ware. This includes items from the bathroom and for the care of invalids.**

# Enoch Wood Sporting Series Ewer

**Description:** An Enoch Wood and Sons "Sporting Series" ewer, c.1820, printed with a wrap-around scene of goats in a landscape, but more importantly, a Royal rat catcher. The rat catcher wears a sash decorated with rats and a crown, and was probably a rat catcher for George III. He sits proudly with his donkey, his ferret, and a dead rat. Ferrets are extremely rare animals to find on transferware. This series was mainly produced on dinner ware and was made for the American export market.
**Size:** 11" (28cm) tall.
**Marks:** Two blue printed "1s."

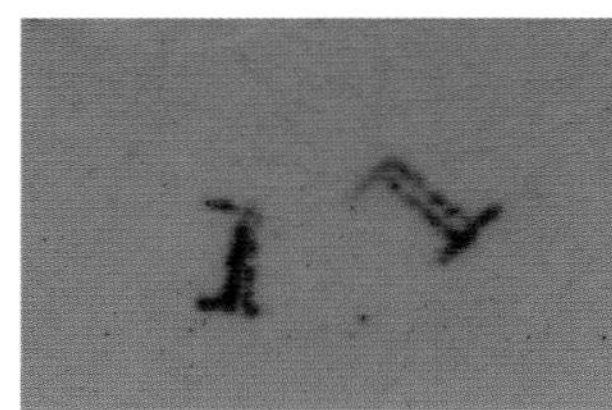

# Enoch Wood Sporting Series Washbowl

**Description:** An Enoch Wood and Sons "Sporting Series" washbowl, c.1820, printed with a scene of a beaver taken from *The Cabinet of Quadrupeds* by John Church, 1805. Behind the central beaver, you can see three beavers gnawing at the base of a tree. Also in the background you can count seven or eight beaver lodges. This series was mainly produced on dinner ware and was made for the American export market.

**Size:** 12.5" (32cm) in diameter.

**Marks:** Impressed Enoch Wood & Sons.

# Brameld Boys Fishing Pattern Soap Box

**Description:** A Brameld "Boys Fishing" pattern soap box and cover, c.1825, well printed with part of the pattern on the lid and another part on the interior. The mother and child are printed on the lid and the two boys fishing in the river are printed on the draining section of the box. It has the border print around the outside. It has a most unusual feature in that the draining section is fixed and is not removable. Most soap boxes have removable draining sections.
**Size:** 4.75" (12cm) long, 2.5" (6.5cm) tall.
**Marks:** Unmarked.

# Spode Broseley Suckling Pot

**Description:** A Spode "Broseley" pattern suckling pot, c.1820. This widely-used pattern was taken from a Chinese original design. It is printed on a bone china body and would originally have had a lid. A suckling pot was used to feed a baby in the early months. They are rarely seen in transferware and this may be because they were broken while in use?

**Size:** 4" (10cm) tall, 5.25" (13.5cm) handle to spout.

**Marks:** Unmarked.

# Stevenson Pastoral Courtship Toothbrush Box

**Description:** A Stevenson "Pastoral Courtship" toothbrush box and cover, c.1825. This pattern shows a shepherd and woman with basket. Note how this example is a slight variation on the standard "Pastoral Courtship" print; the woman with a basket is standing and the shepherd is lying down in this version. Often there is some confusion as to the use of these boxes. Some were for toothbrushes and some were for razors. There can be no argument with this example though; note how the handle is in the form of a toothbrush complete with bristles and handle.
**Size:** 8.75" (22cm) long, 3.25 (9cm) wide.
**Marks:** Unmarked.

# Chinaman with Rocket Ointment Flask

**Description:** A "Chinaman with Rocket" ointment flask, c.1815. This pattern was taken from an original Chinese design and shows a man on a bridge with a closed parasol which looks rather like a rocket. These flasks were used to both store and dispense a wide variety of ointments and potions. Some of these flasks had pottery lids with an integral cork stopper and some simply had a cork stopper. Note the beautiful floral print used on this example to fill the space between the "Chinaman with Rocket" print.
**Size:** 5.5" (14cm) tall, 2" (5cm) in diameter.
**Marks:** Unmarked.

# Patch Stand

**Description:** An extremely rare patch stand, c.1815, decorated with a print of two bird's eggs in a nest. In the eighteenth and nineteenth centuries, the wearing of small patches on the face was commonplace. This was partly to cover up facial marks, especially pox marks, but was also very fashionable. This stand would allow the wearer to have easy access to their patches in front of a mirror so that they could be placed where desired.

**Size:** 3.5" (8.5cm) in diameter, 1" (2.5cm) tall.

**Marks:** Unmarked.

# Spode Caramanian Three-piece Soap Box

**Description:** A Spode "Caramanian" three-piece soap box, c.1810, printed on all three pieces with the "Caramanian" series border print. This consists of a man riding an elephant, a man leading a horse, a rhinoceros, and two cows. The two cows were taken from "A Tiger Prowling through a Village" from a published work *Oriental Field Sports* by T. Williamson, 1807. Note the finely punched holes in the base of the centre section which would allow the soap to drain itself of water. Soap boxes are quite scarce at this period, especially in a pattern such as "Caramanian."

**Size:** 3.75" (9.5cm) in diameter, 3.5" (9cm) tall.

**Marks:** Blue printed Spode.

# Spode Musicians Slop Pail & Cover

**Description:** A Spode "New Shape" slop pail and cover, c.1820, printed with a rare pattern called the "Musicians." This pattern is made up of six musically themed panels that sit around a central panel of musicians. Slop pails are another object that don't survive too well as they must have been awkward to handle when they were full, especially when they were being carried up and down staircases. Note that the holes in the lid of this example are later additions when someone has tried to make this into a potpourri.

**Size:** 12.75" (32.5cm) wide, 12.5" (32cm) tall.

**Marks:** Blue printed SPODE.

# Perfume Flask

**Description:** A small perfume flask printed with a scene of a fisherman before a bridge on both sides. Note the wonderful moulding, especially to the centre of the flask. Perfume flasks were to hold various perfumes and potions of the time, and this example would originally have had a cork stopper.
**Size:** 2.75" (7cm) including the spout.
**Marks:** Unmarked.

# Tower Pattern Suckling Pot

**Description:** A Copeland Late Spode "Tower" pattern upright suckling pot, c.1850. This pattern was taken from a published work *Views of Rome and its Vicinity* by J. Merigot and R. Edwards, 1796-98, and is entitled "Ponte Salaro." A suckling pot was used to feed a baby in the early months and you can imagine that these types of pots were easily dropped and broken. As such, not too many have survived. Although this item is out of the timeline of this book, it is sufficiently rare and interesting to be included.

**Size:** 3.5" (9cm) tall, 4.5" (11.5cm) handle to spout.

**Marks:** Blue printed Copeland Late Spode.

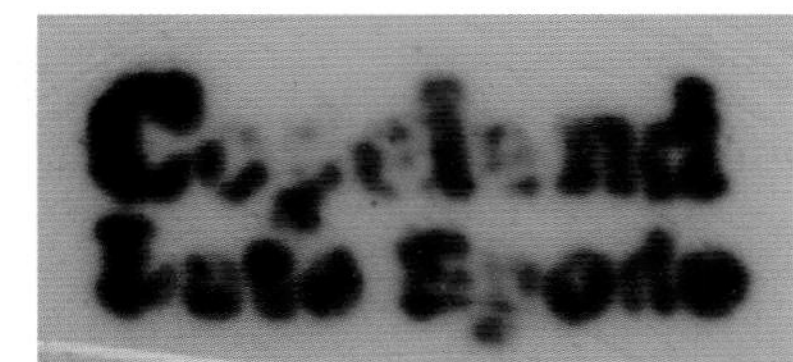

# Large Spode Tower Sponge Box

**Description:** A Spode "Tower" pattern sponge box and cover, c.1825. This pattern was taken from a published work *Views of Rome and its Vicinity* by J. Merigot and R. Edwards, 1796-98 and is entitled "Ponte Salaro." It is a large box with a removable dished lid that allows a sponge to drain into the base section. Note how it has really large holes to make sure the sponge drains as quickly and as efficiently as possible. This shape and style of sponge box is quite uncommon.

**Size:** 11" (28cm) handle to handle, 4" (10cm) tall.

**Marks:** Blue printed SPODE.

# Don Pottery Pap Boat

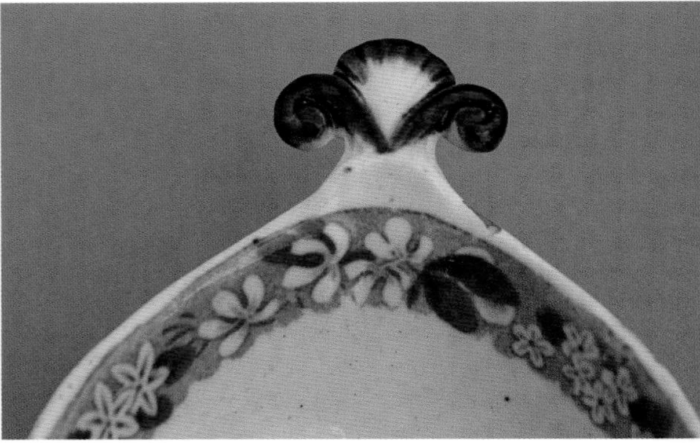

**Description:** A Don Pottery pap boat, c.1825, well printed with a partial scene within a floral border taken from the "Sicilian" and "Italian Views" series. Note the beautifully moulded scroll handle with shell centre. Pap was usually made from bread or flour boiled in water with added butter or sugar. It was then fed to either infants or invalids.
**Size:** 5.75" (14.5cm) long.
**Marks:** Unmarked.

# Spode Milkmaid Screw-top Box

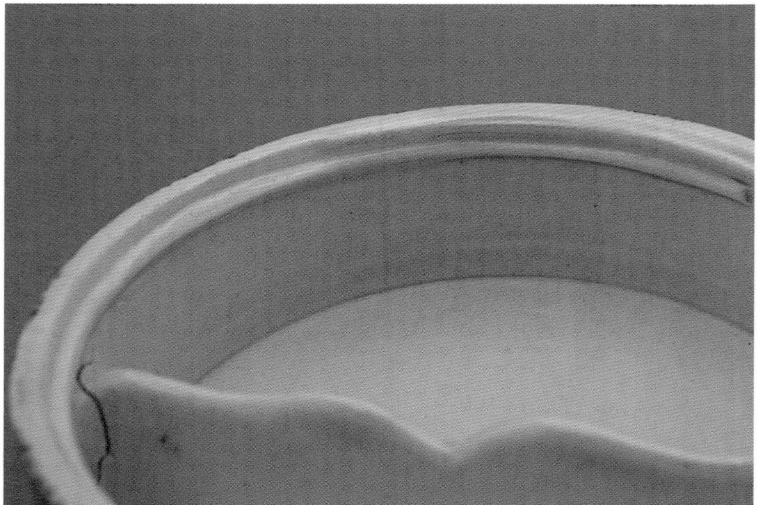

**Description:** A clever Spode "Milkmaid" pattern screw-top box and cover, c.1825, well printed with a scene of a milkmaid milking a cow in a landscape. This box has a moulded screw thread which allows the top to be screwed into place. It was probably for holding powders or patches and would be found on a dressing table. The secure lid prevented the contents from escaping. Note the divider in the box too.
**Size:** 4.75" (12cm) in diameter, 2" (5cm) tall.
**Marks:** Unmarked.

# Sundial Pattern Toothbrush Box

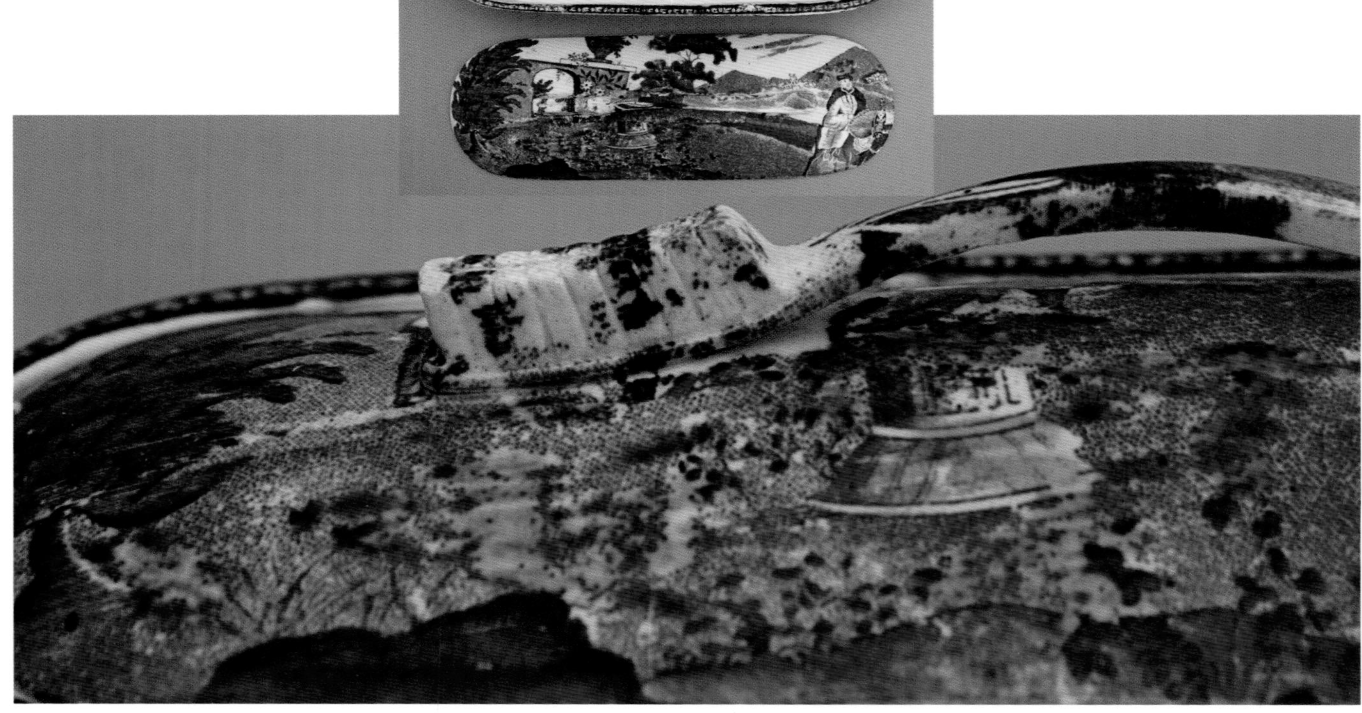

**Description:** A "Sundial" pattern toothbrush box and cover, c.1825, printed with a scene of a man on a donkey and passing a sundial. Some boxes were for toothbrushes and some were for razors, but this example is definitely for toothbrushes; note how the handle is in the form of a toothbrush complete with bristles and handle.
**Size:** 8.25" (21cm) in length.
**Marks:** Unmarked.

# Spode Eye Bath

**Description:** A very rare Spode eye bath, c.1817, printed with partial prints of the "Queen Charlotte" pattern including an island scene on one side and, the most recognisable part of the pattern, the man on a bridge on the other. There are actually two men on the bridge in the standard pattern, but there seems to have been room for only one on this tiny object. It has a shell-moulded edge to the rim and a beautifully moulded stem. There is a blue painted line around the foot that somehow just seems to "finish" it off nicely. Eye baths were used for bathing eyes that were unwell. Eye baths are rare in transferware and are highly-prized by collectors, especially examples like this Spode piece.
**Size:** 3" (7.5cm) tall.
**Marks:** Blue printed SPODE.

# Spode Musicians Pattern Footbath

**Description:** A Spode footbath, c.1820, printed with a rare pattern called the "Musicians." This pattern is made up of six musically themed panels that usually sit around a central panel of musicians. In the case of this footbath, it is decorated with just the six panels. Footbaths were usually accompanied by a large matching jug which would hold the water prior to adding to the footbath to bathe feet.
**Size:** 19" (48cm) handle to handle, 8.25" (21cm) tall.
**Marks:** Printed and impressed SPODE.

# Leeds Screw-top Box

**Description:** A Leeds screw-top box and cover, c.1825, printed to both sides with a pattern called "Scene After Claude Lorraine." This pattern shows a rural Italianate scene of figures on a river before a large ruin. This box has a moulded screw thread which allows the top to be screwed into place. It was probably for holding powders or patches and would be found on a dressing table. The secure lid prevented the contents from escaping.
**Size:** 3" (7.5cm) in diameter.
**Marks:** Unmarked.

# Ridgway Toothbrush Box & Cover

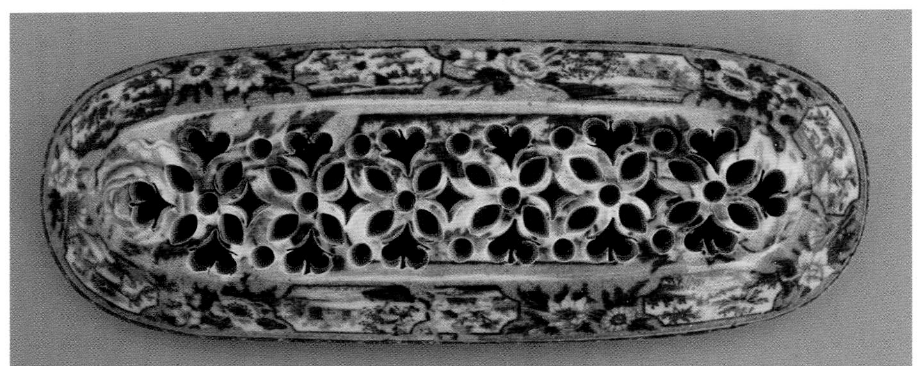

**Description:** A Ridgway "Angus Seat" series toothbrush box and cover, c.1815, printed all over with the border print from this series of landscape views. This border is made up of several cartouches of rural scenes in between large flowers. The lid has various, superb cut-out shapes, including hearts and flowers. This was to allow the toothbrush to dry and be more hygienic. This form of toothbrush box is most unusual. Some examples have one or two holes pierced into the lid, but few are as intricate as this example.
**Size:** 7" (18cm) long.
**Marks:** Unmarked.

# Spode Leech Jar

**Description:** An extremely rare Spode "Tower" pattern leech jar, c.1825. This pattern was taken from a published work *Views of Rome and its Vicinity* by J. Merigot and R. Edwards, 1796-98, and is entitled "Ponte Salaro." Leeches were a very important part of medicine at the time this jar was made. The use of leeches in medicine, or Hirudotherapy as it is known, dates back more than 2,500 years. They were used for blood letting and for cleaning the tissues after surgical operations. This vessel had a pierced lid to stop the leeches from escaping, while allowing them to breath.
**Size:** 9.25" (23.5cm) in diameter, 12.5" (32cm) tall.
**Marks:** Blue printed SPODE.

# Spode Oblong Open Soap Box

**Description:** A Spode "Tower" pattern oblong open soap box, c.1825. This pattern was taken from a published work *Views of Rome and its Vicinity*, J. Merigot and R. Edwards, 1796-98 and is entitled "Ponte Salaro." This soap box has a removable tray that is pierced with many holes to aid the draining process. This shape and size of soap box is very scarce.

**Size:** 6.75" (17cm) long, 3.75" (9.5cm) wide, 2.5" (6.5cm) tall.

**Marks:** Blue printed SPODE.

# Spode Greek Pattern Muffineer

**Description:** A Spode "Greek" pattern muffineer, c.1815, printed with two vases and two panels from the "Greek" series amongst a grapevine sheet pattern background. The vases are both taken from a published work, *The Complete Collection of Antiquities from the cabinet of Sir William Hamilton* by D'Hancarville, 1767, Vol I, Pl. 72. A muffineer by definition is a vessel with a perforated top to be used as a shaker. This example was probably intended to be used to powder wigs, but could also have been used for other similar purposes.

**Size:** 5.5" (14cm) tall.

**Marks:** Indistinct workman's mark.

# Spode Dry Drug Jar

**Description:** An extremely rare Spode dry drug jar, c.1825, printed with the "Union Wreath Second" pattern and has a black painted title of "CERAT: SAPONIS," a hard vegetable wax used in plasters and bandages. This is one of only twenty Spode drug jars made, all for the London firm of Corbyn, Stacey & Co, a wholesale and manufacturing chemist and druggist. At this time, the firm's domestic trade was huge and its export business was growing at a rapid rate. It was not long before they had outlets in Boston, Connecticut, New York, Rhode Island, and Philadelphia.

**Size:** 7.5" (19cm) tall, 6" (15cm) in diameter.

**Marks:** Blue printed SPODE.

# Grazing Rabbits Razor Box

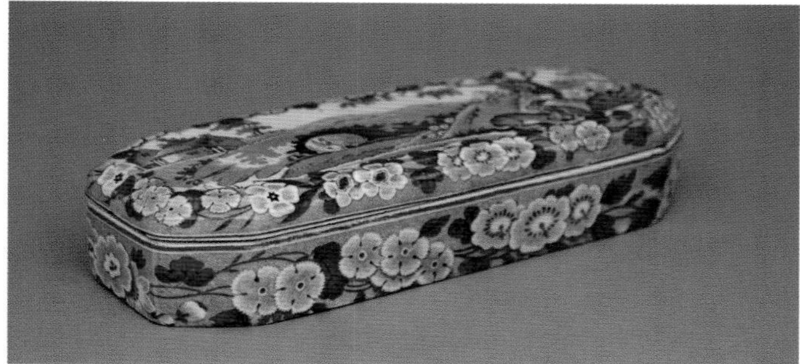

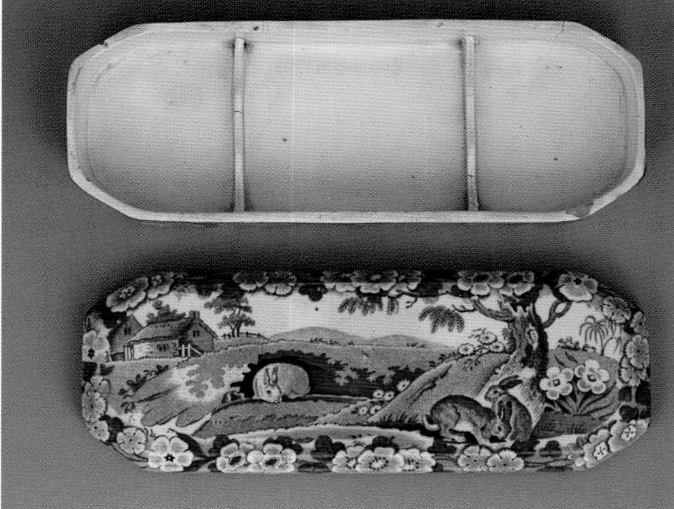

**Description:** A "Grazing Rabbits" pattern razor box and cover, c.1825. This delightful rural scene of three rabbits in a landscape was produced on dinner wares as well as toilet wares. A razor box in this pattern is an uncommon find. Razor boxes were as the name suggests, to keep a cut-throat razor in. This would not only keep it safe from getting lost or blunted, but would also stop it from being played with by children, with potentially dreadful consequences.

**Size:** 7" (18cm) long.

**Marks:** Unmarked.

# Spode Tower Ball Soap Cup

**Description:** An extremely rare Spode "Tower" pattern ball-shaped soap cup, c.1825. This pattern was taken from a published work *Views of Rome and its Vicinity* by J. Merigot and R. Edwards, 1796-98 and is entitled "Ponte Salaro." It has a white, bulbous pedestal foot which has an inner reservoir-like chamber. This would allow the small soap ball to drain and dry. There have been many other uses suggested for this object over the years, but this seems the most likely.

**Size:** 3.25" (8cm) tall, 2.5" (6.5cm) in diameter.

**Marks:** Blue printed SPODE and workman's mark.

# Giant Winemakers Footbath Jug

**Description:** A huge "Winemakers" pattern footbath jug, c.1820, beautifully printed with a wonderful scene of women and cherubs gathering and bringing grapes to the press. A man is treading the grapes and wine is seen to be flowing from the bottom of the press. The jug has a wide grapevine border and an acanthus leaf moulded handle under the spout to aid pouring. This jug would have accompanied a footbath originally and would have been used to carry and store the water prior to it being added to the footbath in which the feet were bathed. The sheer size of the print on this jug suggests that it was specifically engraved for this jug which was no small task!
**Size:** 14" (36cm) tall, 15.5" (39cm) handle to spout.
**Marks:** Unmarked.

# Spode Tower Pattern Bedpan

**Description:** A Spode "Tower" pattern bedpan, c.1820. This pattern was taken from a published work *Views of Rome and its Vicinity* by J. Merigot and R. Edwards, 1796-98, and is entitled "Ponte Salaro." Bedpans were used specifically by bedridden patients. The handle is hollow, and was used to empty the bedpan of its contents.

**Size:** 15.75 (40cm) long including the handle.

**Marks:** Blue printed SPODE.

# Spode Old Peacock Pattern Footbath & Jug

**Description:** A Spode footbath and matching jug, c.1830. The pattern name "Old Peacock" was given by Leonard Whiter, although there is no factory record of this name. Robert Copeland suggested that the birds are Ho-ho birds and that the design may have been taken from Japanese porcelain. Footbaths and jugs would hold water to bathe the feet. This pattern should be considered an extreme rarity; only ten or so examples are known.

**Size:** Jug 12" (30.5cm) tall, Footbath 19" (48cm) wide.

**Marks:** Printed and impressed SPODE.

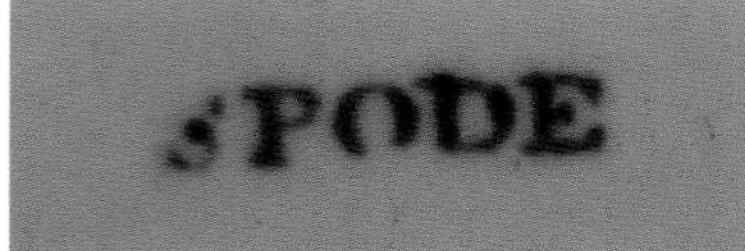

Chapter 5

# Child's Ware, Miniatures, and Toy Ware

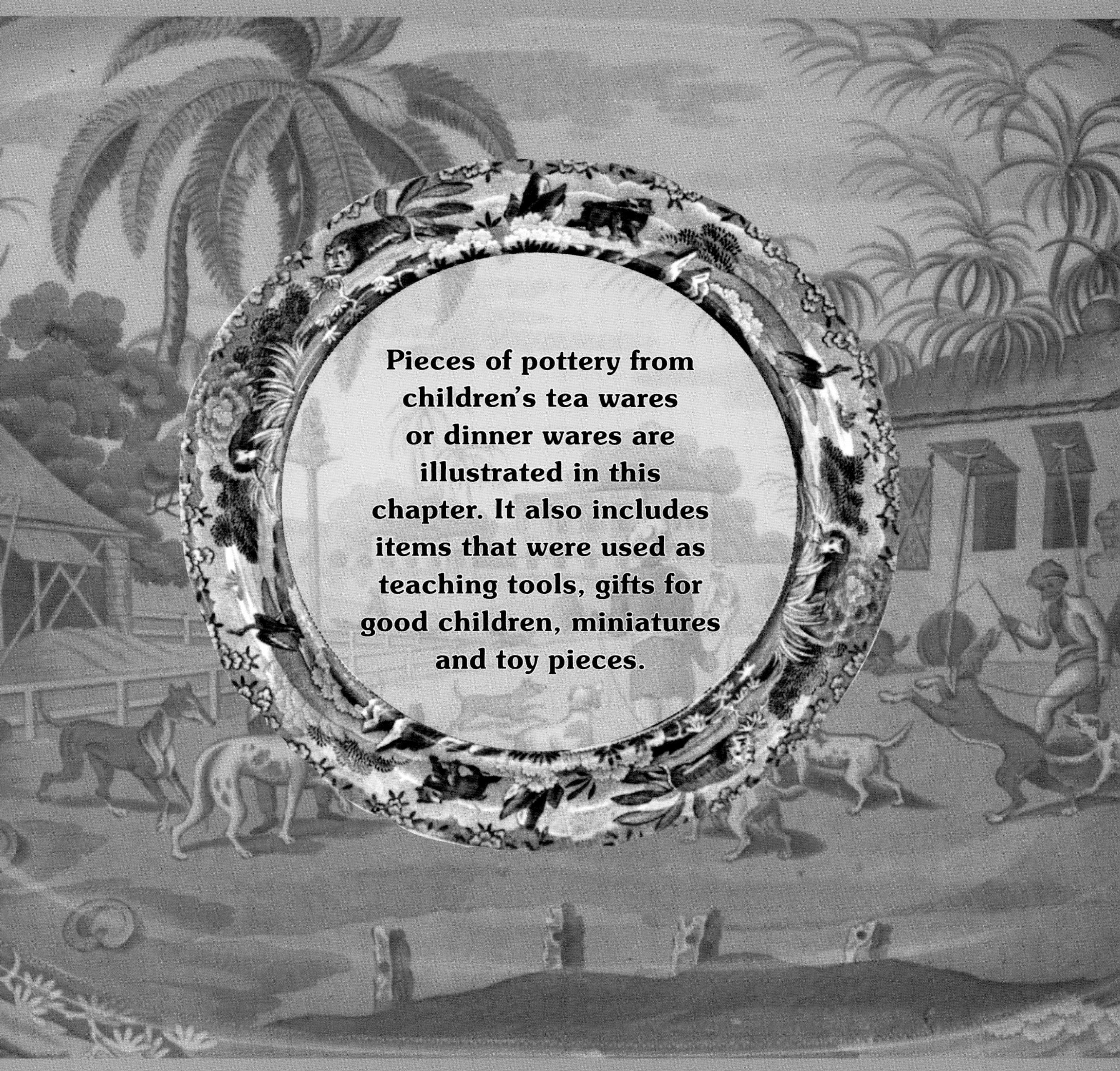

**Pieces of pottery from children's tea wares or dinner wares are illustrated in this chapter. It also includes items that were used as teaching tools, gifts for good children, miniatures and toy pieces.**

# Bewick Child's Teapot

**Description:** A child's teapot with two animal prints, c.1820, decorated with titled prints of a squirrel and a ferret. This teapot is only one of a handful of known pieces of transferware that are printed with a ferret. The source for both prints was *A General History of Quadrupeds*, by Thomas Bewick, 1790. Note the very distinctive vermicelli background used around the panels, which is often seen on pottery produced in Yorkshire.
**Size:** 5" (13cm) long, 4.75" (14cm) tall.
**Marks:** Unmarked.

# Resting Farm Boy Pickle Dish

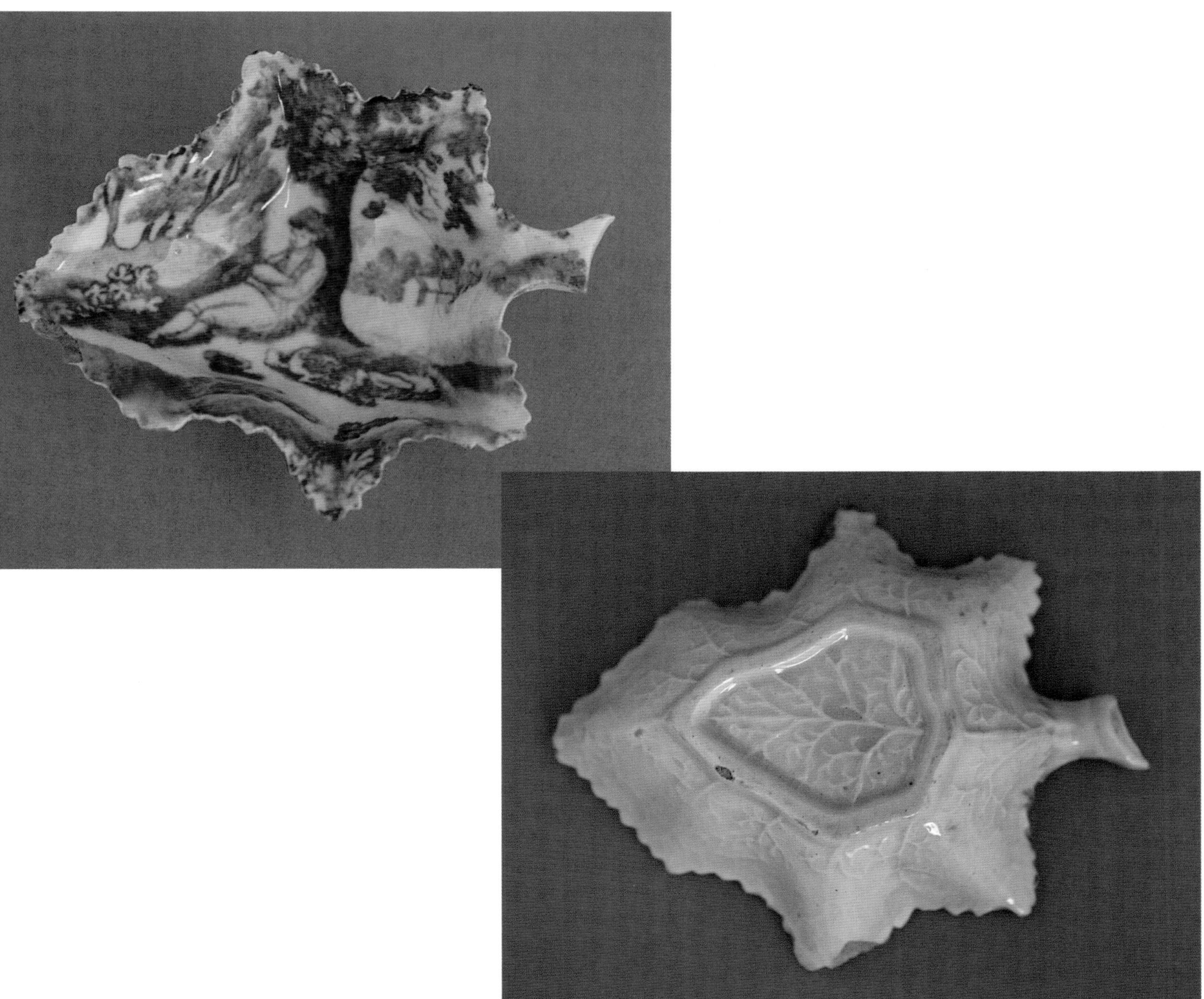

**Description:** A most unusual "Resting Farm Boy" pattern pickle dish, c.1820. The print shows a boy lying under a tree and his dog is asleep next to him. It almost looks as if the boy is playing a pipe. His hat is on the ground in front of him, so could he possibly be busking? The curious thing about this pickle dish is the size. Most pickle dishes are about 6" (15cm) in length, but this one is less than half that size. It was, therefore, almost certainly a toy piece as it would be too small to serve any pickles or condiments. Note the crisply moulded faux leaf veins to the underside.
**Size:** 2.8" (7cm) long.
**Marks:** Unmarked.

# Spode Filigree Chamber Pot & Razor Box

**Description:** A Spode "Filigree" (border print only) pattern toy chamber pot and matching razor box (no lid), c.1825. These small and delicate objects were originally part of a complete toy wash set and must have been extremely vulnerable to being broken or, especially, being lost. It is not entirely clear what their purpose was. Some think they were for children to play with and others believe that they were for adults to display to their friends as conversation pieces.
**Size:** Chamber pot 2.75" (7cm) long. Razor box 2.25" (6cm) long.
**Marks:** Blue printed SPODE.

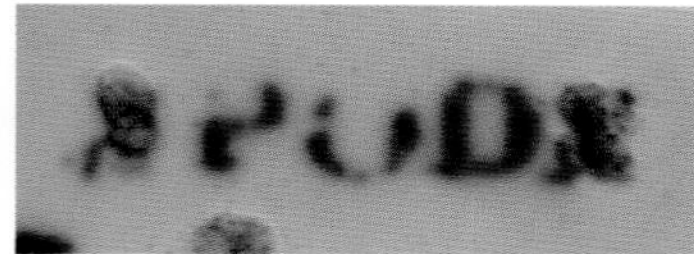

# Don Pottery Turkey Pattern Plate and Teapot

**Description:** A Don Pottery "Turkey" pattern plate and teapot from a child's service, c.1820, printed with two turkeys taken from *A General History of Quadrupeds*, by Thomas Bewick, 1790. Note how the engraver has taken a turkey from the background of the source print and put it in the foreground. Child's pieces don't seem to survive that well and with good reason!

**Size:** Plate 5.25" (13.5cm) in diameter. Teapot 5.5" (14cm) long.

**Marks:** Blue printed Don Pottery.

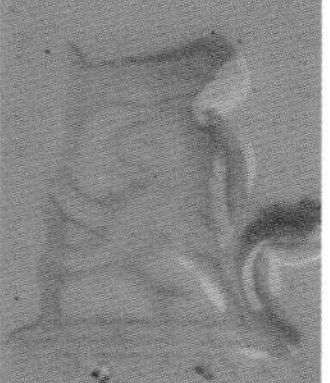

# Child's Mug Little Robin Redbreast

**Description:** A child's mug, c.1825, well printed with a scene of a bird in a tree above the title "LITTLE ROBIN REDBREAST." The bird in the print doesn't look much like a robin, but is very sweet all the same. Mugs like these were used as gifts for good children and as educational aids.

**Size:** 2" (5cm) tall.

**Marks:** Unmarked.

# BRAMELD CHILDREN PLAYING SOUP TUREEN

**Description:** A Brameld "Children Playing" series soup tureen, c.1825, printed with two separate scenes. One shows a boy feeding a horse in a landscape and the other has two children playing with a wheelbarrow before a cottage. Note the use of the vermicelli border around the foot and lid. Also note the distinctive Brameld handle sheet print.

**Size:** 5.75" (14.5cm) wide, 4.25" (11cm) tall.

**Marks:** Unmarked.

# Child's Mug Cheetah

**Description:** A delightful child's mug, c.1825, printed with a cheetah above the word "CHETAH." Note how the name of this animal is misspelled. Not a great educational tool one would say!
**Size:** 2.5" (6cm) tall.
**Marks:** Unmarked.

# Child's Plate Gathering Fruit

**Description:** A child's plate, c.1820, well printed with a titled scene of a mother and child "GATHERING FRUIT." The pattern shows a boy up a tree throwing down apples to his waiting mother below. She is catching the apples in her apron. If you look carefully, you can see that an apple is in mid-flight. The border of the plate is crisply moulded in three pairs which are separated by a butterfly and other symbols. These pairs are; a fox and a hound, a dog and a monkey eating a piece of fruit, and a dog alongside cherubs on a horse-drawn cart.

**Size:** 5.75" (14.5cm) in diameter.

**Marks:** Unmarked.

# Educational Alphabet Puzzle Mug

**Description:** A simply superb alphabet mug, c.1815, printed with an intertwined and rather complicated design made up of the letters of the alphabet. Beneath this it reads "THE ENGLISH ALPHABET." This was probably made as an educational puzzle for children. It is printed with a chinoiserie border to the interior.
**Size:** 3.75" (9.5cm) tall.
**Marks:** Unmarked.

# Brameld Children At Play Teapot

**Description:** A Brameld "Children at Play" pattern child's teapot, c.1810, printed with two different scenes, taken from a Francesco Bartolottzi print, c.1790-95, of three children playing with a goat and a child running. These innocent looking scenes have also been said to represent the sacrifice of a goat.

**Size:** 5.75" (14.5cm) long, 4.25" (11cm) tall.

**Marks:** Unmarked.

# Sign Language Mug

**Description:** A sign language child's mug, c.1820. This little mug is printed with a series of panels that indicate the correct signing for each letter of the alphabet. Sign language is said to date back to the fifth century BC. Note the crisply moulded acanthus leaf terminals to the handle.
**Size:** 2.5" (6.5cm) tall.
**Marks:** Unmarked.

# Pair of Children's Mugs

**Description:** A superb pair of children's mugs, c.1820. One is printed with the name "MARY" and the other is printed with the name "ANN." Note the unusual border around each of the name panels, as it looks similar to vermicelli. Pieces like these were often given as gifts to good children. Maybe they were made for sisters or even twins, which would make them particularly unusual.
**Size:** 2" (5cm) tall.
**Marks:** Unmarked.

# Robert Child's Mug

**Description:** A transfer printed mug, c.1825, printed with a wrap-around scene of a prominent bridge with buildings behind. It has the transfer printed name "Robert" on the front and was possibly a child's mug. Note how the printer left a rough hole in the transfer to allow the name to be transferred onto the mug.
**Size:** 4" (10cm) tall.
**Marks:** Unmarked.

# Miniature Kettle

**Description:** A Dixon, Austin & Co. "Milkmaid and Piping Shepherd" pattern miniature or toy kettle, c.1825. This pattern shows a milkmaid with a bucket on her head. There are cows in a bucolic rural landscape and a shepherd sitting under a tree piping a song. Kettles in pottery are extremely rare and this item is no exception. How the lid has not been lost is a complete mystery.
**Size:** 4" (10cm) wide, 3.5" (9cm) tall.
**Marks:** Unmarked.

Chapter 6

# Commemorative, Named & Dated, and Special Order Ware

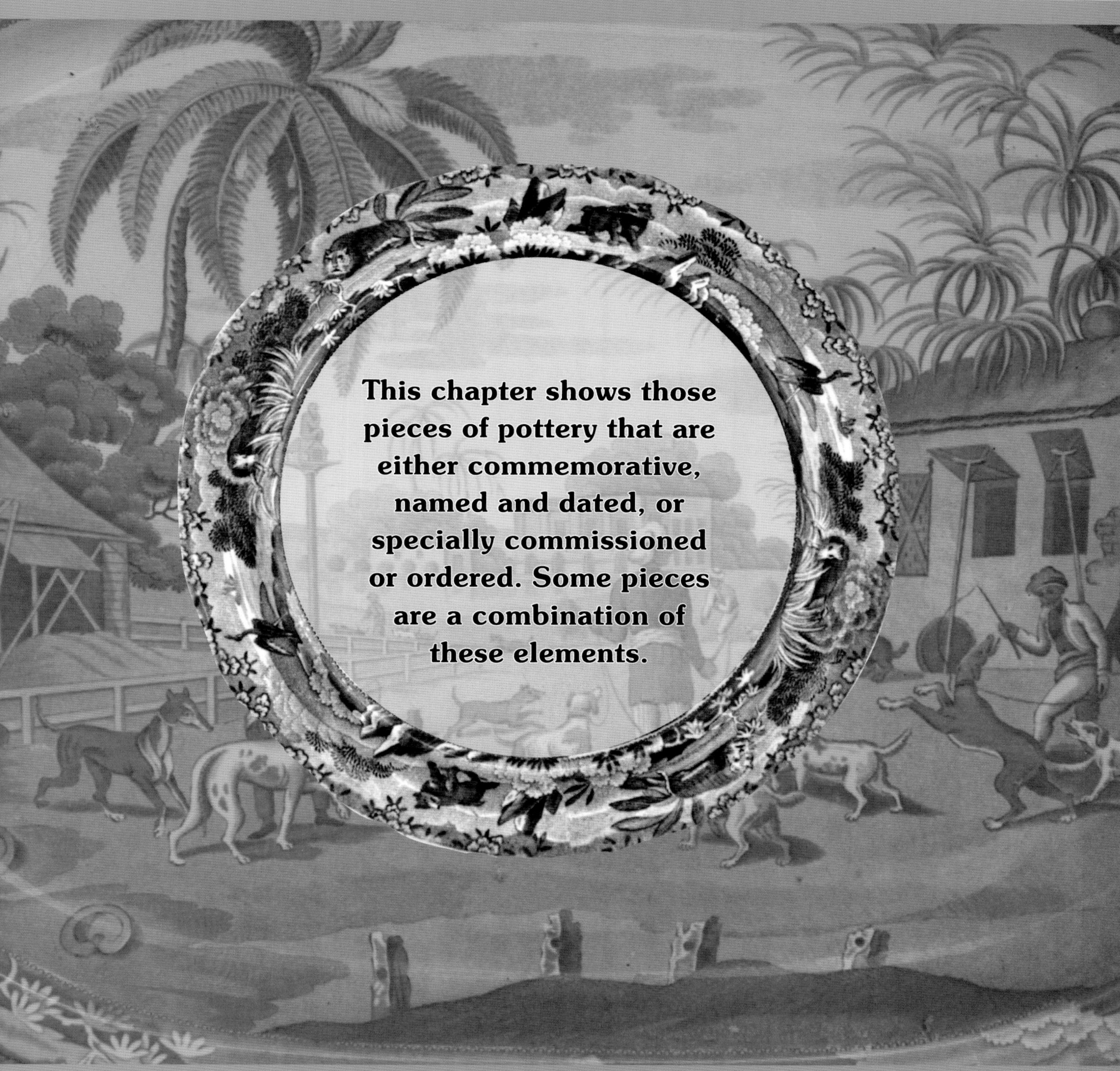

**This chapter shows those pieces of pottery that are either commemorative, named and dated, or specially commissioned or ordered. Some pieces are a combination of these elements.**

# Commemorative Bowl The York

**Description:** A commemorative bowl, c.1804, printed with a wide chinoiserie border to the interior and exterior. The outside is also printed with seven different chinoiserie vignettes. The centre of the bowl is beautifully printed with a sailing vessel and is titled "THE YORK." The *HMS York* was a 64-gun third-rate ship of the line of the Royal Navy. It was launched in 1796, and, in January 1804, it struck Bell Rock in the North Sea off Arbroath. It sank with a total loss of life (491 men). There had been an ongoing debate about Bell Rock and whether it needed a lighthouse, but after this great naval tragedy, an act of Parliament was passed and work began constructing Bell Rock Lighthouse. The lighthouse was built by Robert Stevenson and cost just over £61,000 which was an amazing amount of money at the time.

**Size:** 11.25" (28.5cm) in diameter.

**Marks:** Unmarked.

# Peace of Amiens Jug

**Description:** A Swansea blue printed jug, c.1802., decorated with a pattern called "Peace of Amiens." The pattern shows Britannia in a chariot being drawn by two lions. There is a figure on one of the lions holding a flag that reads "BRITONS REJOICE." There is an angel in the sky holding a banner that reads "May PEACE be Reftored." Under the spout there is a depiction of the city of Amiens and further round there are symbols of peace, plenty, and industry. Britannia is holding two plaques: one reads "GEORGE III For ever," and the other reads "Down with BONAPARTE." The treaty of Amiens was signed in the city of Amiens, 25 March 1802. This treaty temporarily ended hostilities between the French Republic and the United Kingdom during the Napoleonic War, 1793-1815. This peace lasted for just one year and was the only period of harmony between the two nations during the war.
**Size:** 6.75" (17cm) tall.
**Marks:** Unmarked.

# William of Orange Jug

**Description:** A "William of Orange" jug, c.1830, printed with the border from the "Japanese" series and made by Samuel Alcock. Both sides are printed with an image of William III on horseback. Above this image it reads "THE GLORIOUS & IMMORTAL MEMORY." Below this it reads "Strabane Orange Lodge No 250." This lodge is still active in Northern Ireland. Known as William of Orange, William III reigned over England, Ireland, and Scotland (as William II) from 1689 until his death in 1702. He ruled alongside his wife Mary and this period is often referred to as "William and Mary." Note the very unusual spout in the form of a lion's head.
**Size:** 8.75" (22cm) tall.
**Marks:** Unmarked.

# King & Constitution Mug & Bowl

**Description:** A "King and Constitution" mug and footed bowl, c.1793. These two stunning pieces are both printed with a portrait of King George III and Queen Charlotte within a central panel. Above the panel is a crown surrounded by roses and thistles. The panel reads "A KING REVERED, A QUEEN BELOVED, LONG MAY THEY LIVE." The bowl has a wide chinoiserie border to the exterior and interior rims, while the mug has a more modest pattern to the inner rim of flower heads in a geometric design. These were almost certainly produced in 1793 at the outbreak of war with France, following the execution of King Louis XVI.

**Size:** Mug 4.75" (12cm) tall, bowl 10.25" (26cm) in diameter.

**Marks:** Both unmarked.

# Taunton Loving Cup

**Description:** A two-handled loving cup, c.1825, printed with two views of Taunton. One reads "VIEW of the TOWER of St. Mary Magdalenes Church, Taunton." This shows a busy street scene before the church tower. The other side reads "A View of Taunton from a field opposite Playstreet House." This shows a rural view across the river to Taunton. It has a border of flowers, swags, and fruit. Note the dog's head handles. Taunton is a market town that is the county town of Somerset. The name comes from "The town on the River Tone" or "Tone Town" and has been a place of considerable size and importance since Saxon times.
**Size:** 5.25" (13cm) tall, 9.5" (24cm) handle to handle.
**Marks:** Unmarked.

# Queen Victoria Coronation Mug

**Description:** A "Queen Victoria" coronation mug, c.1838, well printed with a portrait of the young Queen Victoria. It has simple floral sprays of the Union flowers (rose, thistle, and shamrock) flanking the portrait and reads "QUEEN VICTORIA." Note that the necklace she is wearing is curved and falls over her shoulder and not in a straight line. This indicates that this mug was produced in Staffordshire and not made in Swansea. She was proclaimed Queen on 20 June 1837, after the death of the then King, William IV. She was crowned Queen on 28 June 1838, at Westminster Abbey. She reigned for 63 years and 7 months until her death in 1901.

**Size:** 2.5" (6.5cm) tall.

**Marks:** Unmarked.

# Death of Nelson Creamer

**Description:** A "Death of Nelson" sparrow-beak creamer from a child's tea service, c.1805, printed with two panels from a pattern that usually has four panels. The two panels shown here are of a lady weeping and a lady holding a vase-shaped lamp. The two missing panels show an angel at a tomb with the word "NELSON" and part of the date of his death "21, 1805," and a panel of Neptune and a ship. Lord Nelson was the first non-Royal person to be given a state funeral. He was laid to rest within a sarcophagus, originally carved for Cardinal Wolsey, in St. Paul's Cathedral, 9 January 1806. The pattern on this creamer has been tentatively attributed to Shorthose.

**Size:** 2" (5cm) tall.

**Marks:** Unmarked.

# Political Electioneering Plate

**Description:** A blue printed electioneering plate, c.1820. Sir Philip Musgrave, Baronet was a Tory candidate, who was finally elected Member of Parliament for Carlisle in 1825. This simple, but elegant plate reads "Sir Philip Musgrave Bart. And the Constitution." There are two printed crossed flags below this inscription. Electioneering commemorative wares are not common.

**Size:** 9.25" (23.5cm) in diameter.

**Marks:** Unmarked.

# Waterloo Cup & Saucer

**Description:** A "Waterloo" cup and saucer, c.1815. Both pieces are well printed with a scene commemorating the end of the reign of Emperor Napoleon and the Napoleonic wars. There were two versions of the pattern made, one with writing in English and one in French. Presumably, these were produced for different markets. This example reads "Le France de la Touronne de Holland" on the gable-end of the central building. The building is said to have been Napoleon's headquarters during the battle of Waterloo. The border has portraits of Wellington and Blücher. They were the leaders of the combined armies of the Seventh Coalition. This was an Anglo-Allied army under the command of the Duke of Wellington combined with a Prussian army under the command of Gebhard von Blücher. The cup in this set has a retailer's mark for "S MARKS" printed to the underside.

**Size:** Saucer diameter, 5.25" (13cm).

**Marks:** Printed retailer's mark.

# Scottish Arts Soup Dish

**Description:** A "Scottish Arts" pattern soup dish, c.1815. Although this example is unmarked, the pattern has been noted with a printed title mark of "Scottish Arts." There is woman to the centre who is holding an unwound scroll. It reads "Wallace, Bruce, Hamilton, Douglas, Buchanan, Murray, Duncan, Abercrombie, Graham." She is flanked by a man in Scottish dress holding a sword and by children bearing an artist's palate, a harp, and an architectural drawing. This pattern possibly commemorates the Scottish achievements in the fields of war, art, and politics.
**Size:** 10" (25.5cm) in diameter.
**Marks:** Unmarked.

# Queen Victoria Coronation Mug

**Description:** A "Queen Victoria" coronation mug, c.1838. This mug was produced in very small numbers to celebrate the coronation of Victoria. It was specially commissioned by the estate of Hoghton Tower, who had a celebration banquet in honour of Victoria on 28 June 1838. These mugs would have been given by the estate to the estate workers' children as a souvenir of the momentous occasion. Hoghton Tower is a sixteenth century English stately home and near Preston in Lancashire. Victoria was proclaimed Queen on 20 June 1837, after the death of King William IV. She was crowned Queen on 28 June 1838, at Westminster Abbey. She reigned for 63 years and 7 months, until her death in 1901.

**Size:** 3" (7.5cm) tall.

**Marks:** Unmarked.

# Shakespeare Mug

**Description:** A "Shakespeare" commemorative mug, c.1830, printed with a design of the great bard on one side, the mulberry tree on the other, and a winged angel opposite the handle. Shakespeare is leaning on a monument whilst holding a passage from "The Tempest." Shakespeare planted his famous mulberry tree in Stratford-upon-Avon in 1609 and was said to have taken the tree from the garden of James I. The border is made up of various panels that depict scenes from Shakespeare's works. William Shakespeare was an English poet and playwright who wrote thirty-eight plays, one hundred fifty-four sonnets, two long narrative poems, and several other poems. He was born and raised in Stratford-upon-Avon and had three children with his wife Anne Hathaway. He died at the age of 52 in 1616.

**Size:** 6.25" (16cm) tall.

**Marks:** Unmarked.

# Swansea Nelson Commemorative Mug

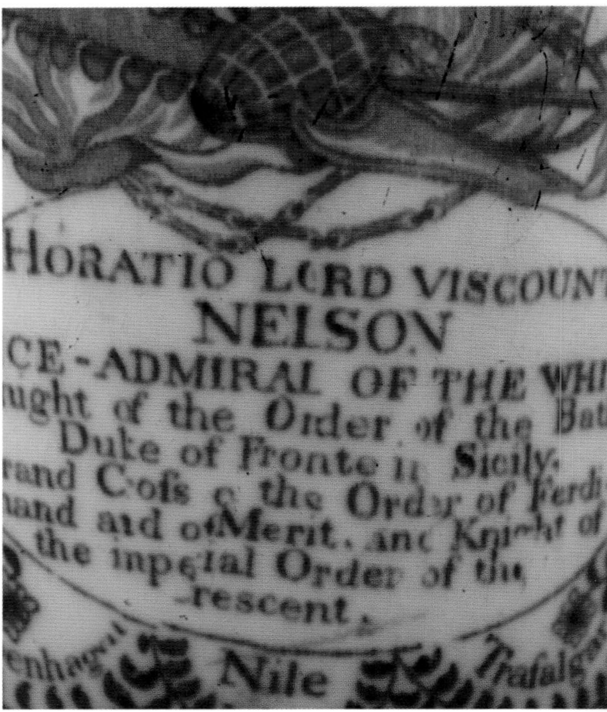

**Description:** A Swansea "Death of Nelson" mug, c.1805, printed with three key elements: firstly, a portrait of Lord Nelson that reads "ENGLAND EXPECTS EVERY MAN TO DO HIS DUTY" and "Shew me my country's Foes, the Hero cry'd: He Saw – He fought – He Conquered – And he di'd;" secondly, a print of *HMS Victory*, Nelson's famous flag ship on which he died on 21 October 1805; thirdly, a panel opposite the handle that reads "HORATIO LORD VISCOUNT NELSON, VICE ADMIRAL OF THE WHITE. Knight of the Order of the Bath. Duke of Bronte in Sicily. Grand C[r]ofs of the Order of Ferdinand and of Merit, and Knight of the inpe[r]ial Order of the [C]rescent." Beneath this it lists his great naval achievements: "Copenhagen," the "Nile," and "Trafalgar."

**Size:** 4.5" (11cm) tall.

**Marks:** Unmarked.

# WELLINGTON & HILL MUG

**Description:** A "Wellington and Hill" mug, c.1815. The mug is printed with three distinct prints. Firstly, a print of Wellington on horseback with sword drawn. There is a banner that reads "THE DUKE of WELLINGTON." The second print is of "LORD HILL" on horseback, also with sword drawn. The third print is made up of flags, a sword, a rifle, a canon, and a drum. The drum bears the initials "GR" which stands for George Rex. This mug was possibly made to commemorate the battle of Waterloo in 1815, but could have also been for any number of the earlier Peninsular campaigns that involved Wellington and Hill. General Rowland Hill, 1st Viscount Hill of Almaraz, served in the Napoleonic Wars as a trusted brigade, division, and corps commander under the command of the Duke of Wellington. He became Commander-in-Chief of the British Army in 1829. Field Marshal Arthur Wellesley, 1st Duke of Wellington, participated in some 60 battles throughout his military career, most famously, restoring peace to Europe at the battle of Waterloo in 1815. He was also Prime Minister from 1828–30 and served briefly in 1834.

**Size:** 4.75" (12cm) tall.

**Marks:** Unmarked.

# Nelson Commemorative Mug

**Description:** A "Death of Nelson" commemorative mug, c.1805, printed with two panels, one of Lord Nelson and one of *HMS Victory*. The Nelson panel reads "ENGLAND EXPECTS EVERY MAN WILL DO HIS DUTY, ADMIRAL LORD NELSON." The HMS Victory panel reads "OFF TRAFALGAR, OCTOBER 21, 1805, VICTORY." These panels sit amongst a stylised floral background.
**Size:** 4.75" (12cm) tall.
**Marks:** Unmarked.

# York Minster Fire Jug

**Description:** A "York Minster Fire" jug, c.1829, printed with a scene of the famous York Minster ablaze to one side and a print of Jonathon Martin to the other. The border is made up of architectural Gothic arches. Jonathon Martin moved to York in 1828. Whilst attending an evening service at the Minster on 1 February, 1829, he was said to have been annoyed by a noise made by the organ. He secreted himself in the Minster and later that night set fire to the woodwork in the choir area. The roof of the central aisle was entirely destroyed from the lantern tower almost to the east window, as was most of the woodwork in the interior, including the organ and its screen, the tabernacle work, the stalls, galleries, bishop's throne, and the pulpit. He was arrested on 5 February and was tried at York Castle. Despite the jury ruling of guilty (which would have resulted in hanging), the judge declared him not guilty on the grounds of insanity. He was detained in Bethlem Royal Hospital, where he died on 26 May 1838.

**Size:** 5" (12.5cm) tall.

**Marks:** Unmarked.

# British Admiralty Commemorative Bowl

**Description:** A British Admiralty commemorative footed bowl, c.1795. The bowl has a chinoiserie border to the interior and exterior. The centre has a panel that reads "May all British ADMIRALS have the Eye of a HAWKE, the Heart of a WOLFE and the spirit of a RODNEY." The names in capitals were famous British officers. Admiral of the Fleet Edward Hawke, 1st Baron Hawke was First Lord of the Admiralty between 1766 and 1771. Wolfe probably refers to Major General James P. Wolfe who was a British Army Officer, 1740-1759. George Brydges Rodney, 1st Baron Rodney was a British Naval officer and later Admiral, 1732–1792. It is interesting that this bowl is asking that British Admirals be great, but one of the names used wasn't an Admiral. Maybe the potters didn't know this or maybe they were very keen to use the word "Wolfe" in the propaganda-like slogan.
**Size:** 7.25" (18.5cm) in diameter.
**Marks:** Unmarked.

# Queen Victoria Coronation Mug

**Description:** A "Queen Victoria" coronation mug, c.1838. This mug was produced in very small numbers and was to celebrate the coronation of Victoria. It was specially commissioned by the town of Preston, Lancashire. It has a portrait of Victoria and reads "QUEEN VICTORIA, CROWNED 28 JUNE 1838, SUCCESS TO THE TOWN AND TRADE OF PRESTON." These short-run local souvenir pieces are extremely scarce. Victoria was proclaimed Queen on 20 June 1837, after the death of King William IV. She was crowned Queen on the 28 June 1838, at Westminster Abbey. She reigned for 63 years and 7 months until her death in 1901. This mug has been noted marked DAVENPORT in the past.
**Size:** 3" (7.5cm) tall.
**Marks:** Unmarked.

# Battle Of Trafalgar Jug

**Description:** A battle of "Trafalgar" jug, c.1805. The pattern on this jug is made up of mermen blowing trumpets on a sea-like background. A pair of mermen each flank a central panel that reads "TRAFALGAR" on a banner above a pyramid and a castle. These represent Admiral Lord Nelson's great victories at the Battle of the Nile (1798), the Battle of Copenhagen (1801), and the battle of Trafalgar (1805), at which Nelson died. The jug has a wide chinoiserie border around the inside and outside of the rim. This jug was produced to commemorate the death of Nelson, but more specifically the victory at Trafalgar in 1805.

**Size:** 6.75" (17cm) tall.

**Marks:** Unmarked.

# Irish Commemorative Saucer

**Description:** An Irish commemorative saucer, c.1829. It shows a scene of a woman holding an Irish flag and a harp. Next to her stands a warrior with a shield and spear. Behind them is a large ecclesiastical building and sun rays breaking through the clouds. This is said to represent Catholic Ireland (woman), Daniel O'Connell (warrior), and Roman Catholic Church (building in background); the sun rays are the possibility of Catholic Emancipation, which became reality in 1829. This pattern has been attributed to the Dudson factory.
**Size:** 5.5" (14cm) in diameter.
**Marks:** Unmarked.

# Sunderland Bridge Frog Mug

**Description:** A Sunderland Bridge frog mug, c.1820, printed with a floral border to the inside which is highlighted with red and green enamels. This border is also found on the "Italian Scenery" pattern. Opposite the handle, there is a very fine and detailed print of the bridge. It reads "A South East View of the STUPENDOUS Iron Bridge built over the River Wear at Sunderland by R. BURDON Esq. MP. Begun 24 Sep. 1793, Opened 9 August 1796. Span of Arch 236 Ft, Height 100 Ft. Cast Iron 214 Tons, Wrought …46." The mug has two frogs inside. Note how the printer has printed the border across the head of one of them. Mugs such as these were made to commemorate the opening of this fine bridge.

**Size:** 6.5" (16.5cm) tall.

**Marks:** Unmarked.

# St. Michael's Mount Mug

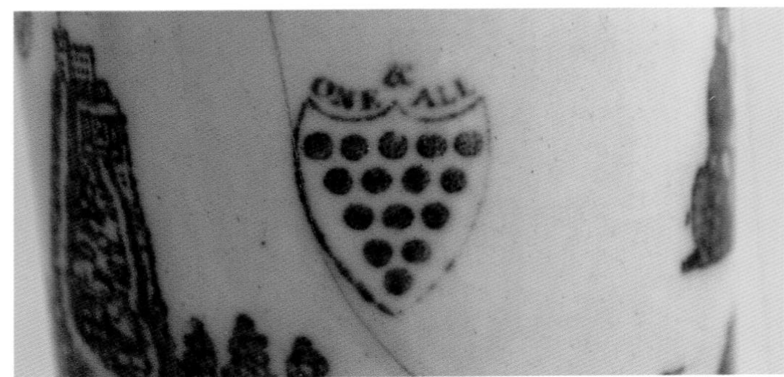

**Description:** A Swansea mug, c.1800, printed to both sides with a view of "ST. MICHAEL'S MOUNT." St. Michael's Mount is a small island located 400 yards (366m) off the Mount's Bay coast of Cornwall. The prints are very detailed showing the castle, the houses, and fishing vessels on the sea. It has a shield with the Cornish motto "ONE & ALL" and a man sitting on a barrel saying "FISH TIN & COPPER." These were used symbolically together as they show the "traditional" three main industries of Cornwall.

**Size:** 4.5" (11.5cm) tall.

**Marks:** Swansea workman's mark.

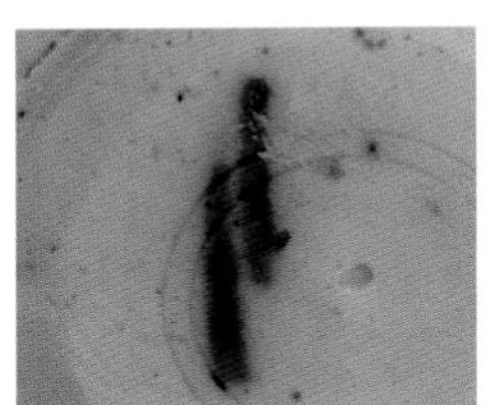

# Dear Tom Mug

**Description:** A "Dear Tom" mug, c.1800, printed with a rotund man enjoying his pipe and jug of ale. There is a table next to him with a candle, tobacco, and spare pipes. Below this print it reads "Dear TOM this Brown JUG." This is the first line from the popular song by Francis Fawkes who wrote about a hearty fellow and drinker whose body, according to the song, was made into a Toby jug drinking vessel after he was dead. The print is thought to represent the notorious Yorkshire man, Henry Elwes, who was known as "Toby Fillpot" (or Philpot) after which the popular vessels were named.
**Size:** 5" (12.5cm) tall.
**Marks:** Unmarked.

# Victoria & Albert Commemorative Soup Dish

**Description:** A "Queen Victoria and Prince Albert" wedding commemorative soup dish, c.1840, printed with the border from the standard "Willow" pattern around the rim. The centre has a printed panel of their portraits. Above them is a crown and the words "QUEEN VICTORIA BORN MAY 24 1819. PRINCE ALBERT BORN AUGUST 26 1819, MARRIED FEB 10th 1840."Queen Victoria proposed to Albert on 15 October 1839 and they were married on 10 February 1840, in the Chapel Royal of St. James's Palace, London. They had nine children together and were married for twenty-one years until his death in 1861.

**Size:** 10.25" (26cm) in diameter.

**Marks:** Unmarked.

# Swansea Duke Of York Mug

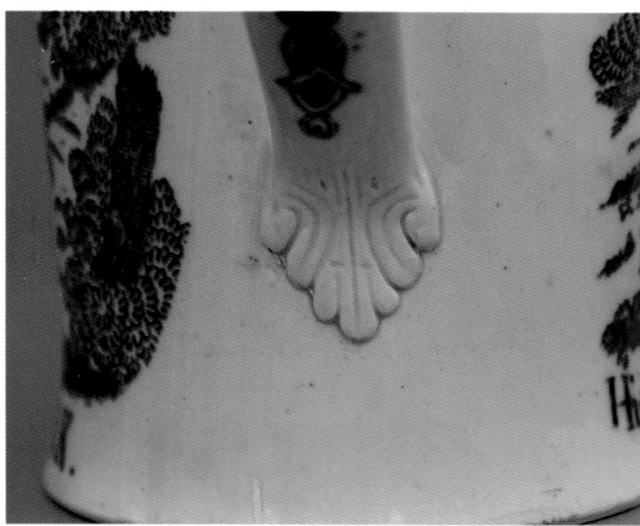

**Description:** A Swansea "Duke of York" mug, c.1800, well printed with a wrap-around scene showing the Duke of York on horseback on a battle field with soldiers and cannons. There is a small town in the background. Prince Frederick, Duke of York and Albany, was the second eldest child and second son of King George III. He was created Duke of York and Albany and Earl of Ulster on 27 November 1784. In 1795, the Duke of York took command of the regular British Army, including the Ordnance Corps, the Militia, and the Volunteers. After the death of his father in 1820 and until his own death in 1827, he was heir presumptive to his elder brother, King George IV.

**Size:** 4.75" (12cm) tall.

**Marks:** Impressed circle to base.

# Davenport Farmer George Soup Dish

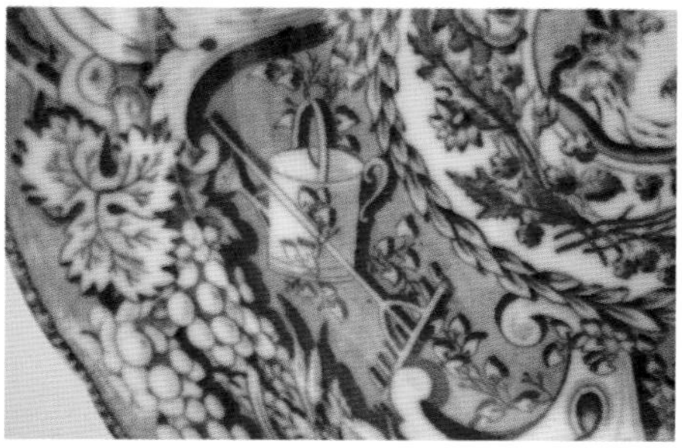

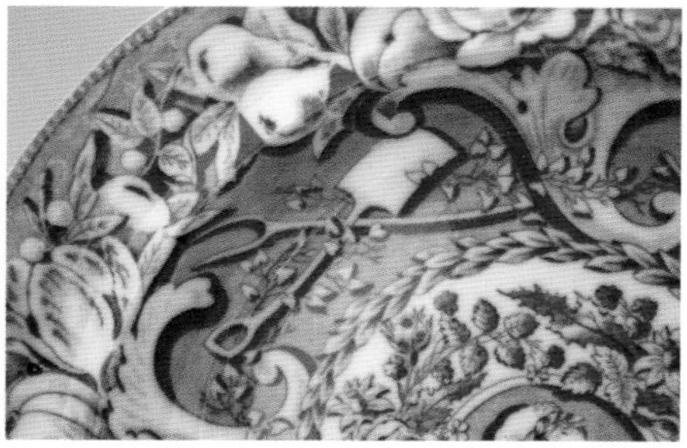

**Description:** A "Farmer George" pattern soup dish, c.1810-15, printed with a bust of George III looking rather like a Roman emperor. The bust is surrounded by the Union flowers of the rose, thistle, and shamrock. The outer section of the pattern is made up of cornucopias of fruits, flowers, crops, and grapes. Between the cornucopias are four panels of different farming implements that include a fork, spade, watering can, rake, plough, and sickle. This border alludes to the somewhat unflattering name that George III had–"Farmer George." This dish may have been made in 1810, to celebrate George's Golden Jubilee, or in 1815, to commemorate the victory at Waterloo and the peace in Europe. The latter would also be supported by the fact that he is wearing a laurel wreath in the pattern which often signifies victory.

**Size:** 10" (25.5cm) in diameter.

**Marks:** Impressed Davenport.

# Queen Caroline Plate

**Description:** A "Queen Caroline" child's plate, c.1821. This superbly moulded plate is decorated with a portrait of Queen Caroline and was probably made at the time of her death in 1821. Caroline of Brunswick-Wolfenbüttel was the Queen consort of King George IV from 29 January 1820 until her death on 7 August 1821. Caroline had married George in 1795, and, between 1795 and 1820, she was Princess of Wales. In 1796, George and Caroline had a baby girl, Princess Charlotte of Wales. In 1814, Caroline left England and moved to Italy and it was widely assumed that she was committing adultery with Bartolomeo Pergami. When George became King in 1820, she returned to Britain to assert her position as Queen. George attempted to divorce her, but failed. The following year, in July 1821, Caroline fell ill after she was barred from the coronation on the orders of her husband. She died three weeks later, and her body was buried in her native Brunswick.

**Size:** 4.75" (12cm) in diameter.

**Marks:** Unmarked.

# Robert Burns Commemorative Plate

**Description:** A commemorative series plate, c.1820. This series is attributed to the Caledonian Pottery, Scotland. The series is very distinctive and is made up of a wide border of Union flowers with a small commemorative centre. This example is printed with a portrait of "ROBERT BURNS." Robert Burns (1759 – 1796) was a Scottish poet and a lyricist. He is widely regarded as the national poet of Scotland and is celebrated worldwide. He famously wrote "Auld Lang Syne" which is sung at Hogmanay/New Year's Eve. He is also known as Rabbie Burns, Scotland's favourite son, the Ploughman Poet, Robden of Solway Firth, and the Bard of Ayrshire. His birthday is still commemorated on Burn's Night on the 25th of January.
**Size:** 10" (25.5cm) in diameter.
**Marks:** Unmarked.

# The Robert Bruce Commemorative Plate

**Description:** A commemorative series plate, c.1820. This series is attributed to the Caledonian Pottery, Scotland. The series is very distinctive and is made up of a wide border of Union flowers with a small commemorative centre. This example is printed with a sailing vessel entitled "THE ROBERT BRUCE." The vessel illustrated is believed to have been launched at Greenock, Scotland in 1817. The ship depicted in this pattern was probably named after Robert the Bruce. He was King of Scots (1306–1329), Earl of Carrick and Lord of Annandale, victor at the Battle of Bannockburn.
**Size:** 10" (25.5cm) in diameter.
**Marks:** Unmarked.

# George III Commemorative Soup Dish

**Description:** A commemorative series soup dish, c.1820. This series is attributed to the Caledonian Pottery, Scotland. The series is very distinctive and is made up of a wide border of Union flowers with a small commemorative centre. This example is printed with George III handing a bible to a small boy. Below this image it reads "I hope the time will come when every poor child in my dominions will be able to read the Bible." George III was King of Great Britain and King of Ireland from 25 October 1760 until the union of these two countries on 1 January 1801, after which he was King of the United Kingdom of Great Britain and Ireland until his death on 29 January, 1820.

**Size:** 9.75" (25cm) in diameter.

**Marks:** Unmarked.

# Queen of England Commemorative Soup Dish

**Description:** A commemorative series soup dish, c.1820. This series is attributed to the Caledonian Pottery, Scotland. The series is very distinctive and is made up of a wide border of Union flowers with a small commemorative centre. This example is printed with a portrait of "THE QUEEN OF ENGLAND." It depicts Queen Charlotte (1744 – 1818), who was Queen consort of the United Kingdom as the wife of King George III. George and Charlotte had fifteen children, the eldest of whom were George (latterly George IV) and Prince Frederick, the Duke of York and Albany. She is the second longest-serving consort in British history.

**Size:** 9.75" (25cm) in diameter.

**Marks:** Unmarked.

# George III Commemorative Soup Dish

**Description:** A commemorative series soup dish, c.1820. This series is attributed to the Caledonian Pottery, Scotland. The series is very distinctive and is made up of a wide border of Union flowers with a small commemorative centre. This example is printed with a portrait of George III. Above and below the portrait it reads "Sacred to the Memory of GEORGE III, Who died 29 Jan, 1820." George III was King of Great Britain and King of Ireland from 25 October 1760 until the union of these two countries on 1 January 1801, after which he was King of the United Kingdom of Great Britain and Ireland until his death on 29 January 1820. He was dubbed "Farmer George" by satirists, at first mocking his interest in mundane matters rather than matters of State, but latterly to show his passionate interest in agriculture.
**Size:** 9.75" (25cm) in diameter.
**Marks:** Unmarked.

# Nelson Commemorative Footed Bowl

**Description:** An Admiral Lord Nelson commemorative bowl, c.1805, printed with a wide chinoiserie pattern to both the exterior and interior rims. The rim has an ochre painted line around its circumference. The centre of the bowl has a beautifully engraved print that reads "ADMIRAL LORD NELSON. ENGLAND EXPECTS EVERY MAN TO DO HIS DUTY." It also has his three most famous battles, "Trafalgar," "Copenhagen," and the "Nile," around the panel. Above and below the panel it reads "Shew me my Country's Foes, The Hero cry'd; He faw — He faught — He conquer'd, And he di'd" and "Dear to his Country, fhall his mem'ry live; But sorrow drowns the joy, His Deeds fhould give." This bowl was produced soon after his death in 1805 to commemorate his life and achievements.

**Size:** 8.75" (22cm) in diameter, 3.25" (8cm) tall.

**Marks:** Unmarked.

# Swansea Guillotine Mug

**Description:** A Swansea "Guillotine" mug, c.1793, well printed with a scene of Louis XVI at his execution. There is a printed caption that reads "View of LA GUILLOTINE or the modern Beheading Machine at Paris. By Which Louis XVI, late King of France, was beheaded Jan, 21, 1793." Louis XVI ruled as King of France from 1774 until 1791, and then as King of the French from 1791 to 1792. Suspended and arrested as part of the insurrection of August 10th, 1792, during the French Revolution, he was tried by the National Convention, found guilty of high treason, and executed by guillotine on 21 January 1793. He is the only king of France ever to be executed. Note how this rather gruesome transfer has Louis looking down into "his" basket; it could have been worse though, it could have been after the blade had fallen!

**Size:** 4.5" (11.5cm) tall.

**Marks:** Swansea workman's mark.

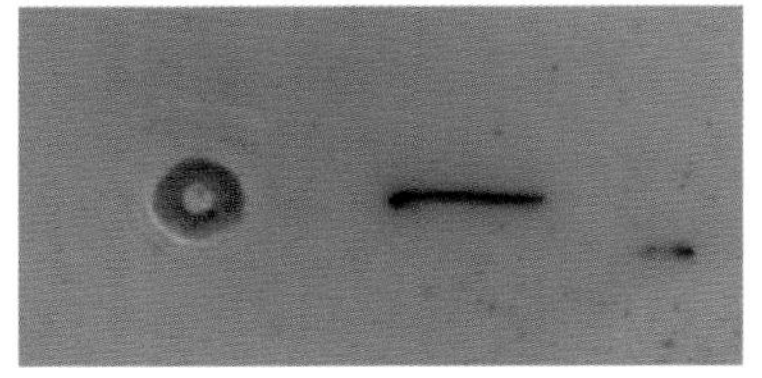

# Villa d'Este Bowl

**Description:** A "Villa d'Este" commemorative washbowl, c.1820. Queen Caroline was Queen consort of George IV. They married in April 1795, but he only agreed to marry her so that Parliament would increase his allowance, as he was heavily in debt. After a somewhat troubled marriage, in 1814, Caroline left Great Britain and met Count Bartolomeo Pergami on a trip to Italy. She hired him as head of household. In 1815, Caroline bought Villa d'Este on Lake Como. She and Pergami would cruise around the Mediterranean together, and rumours started that they were having an adulterous relationship. In 1820, George tried to get Parliament to pass the Pains and Penalties Bill to strip Caroline of her title of Queen consort, but failed. George became King in early 1820, but at the coronation on 19 July, 1821, he would not allow Caroline to take part in the ceremony. She died soon after on the 7 August 1821.

**Size:** 12" (30.5cm) in diameter.

**Marks:** Unmarked.

# Named & Dated Duke of York Jug

**Description:** A named and dated commemorative jug, c.1794, printed with a wide chinoiserie border and two mirrored chinoiserie landscape scenes. Under the spout is has the name and date "Thomas Holbrook, 1794." Beneath this, there is a well-engraved print of the Duke of York and the words "His Royal Highnefs, The Duke of York." The Duke of York, depicted here, was Prince Frederick Augustus, Duke of York and Albany, and the second eldest child of George III. The foot of this jug has a print around it that has been noted on a Davenport pattern "Chinoiserie Fishermen." On that basis, this jug is tentatively attributed to Davenport.

**Size:** 9.5" (24cm) tall.

**Marks:** Unmarked.

# Boy On A Buffalo Named & Dated Jug

**Description:** A huge chinoiserie named and dated jug, c.1796, printed with two large prints of the "Boy on a Buffalo" pattern. This pattern is a very famous design and shows a boy riding a large buffalo across a chinoiserie landscape. The jug is also printed with ten prints of floral sprays and has a wide border that includes moths or butterflies. Below the spout, there is a wonderful hand painted rhyme that includes a name and date. It reads "Who lies here / Why do you think / poor Earthen ware / come give him some drink / what a dead man drink / A good reason why / For when he was alive / he was allways dry / William Mofs / 1796." The script is beautifully painted and was clearly done by a very skilled person.
**Size:** 13" (33cm) tall.
**Marks:** Unmarked.

# Swansea Jug

**Description:** A superb Swansea floral jug with motto, c.1800, printed with two large and two small floral spays to the body and a border print that is often found on a Cambrian pattern called the "Precarious Chinaman." The front of the jug is printed with a motto that reads "Sit down & spend a Social hour / In harmlefs mirth & fun / Let Friendship reign be just & Kind / And evil speak of none."
**Size:** 7" (18cm) tall.
**Marks:** Blue printed workman's mark.

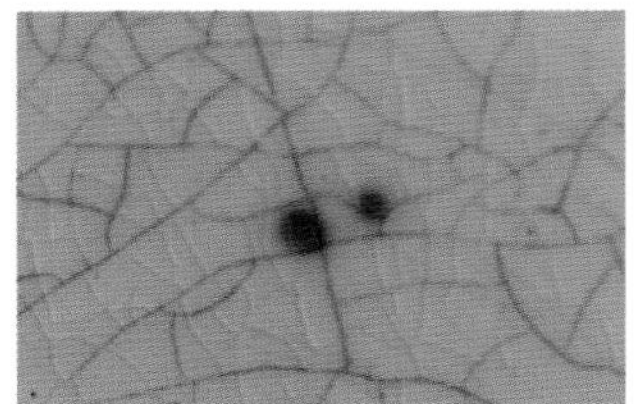

# Villagers Pattern Named & Dated Jug

**Description:** A large "Villagers" pattern named and dated jug, c.1833. This pattern was produced by Turner, Heathcote, and Marsh, but they all had ceased production when this jug was made in c.1833. There have been examples of the "Villagers" pattern marked "JONES" and they were potting in 1833 at the Villa Pottery, Cobridge, so this jug is tentatively attributed to them. The front of the jug has a purple lustre shield flanked by corn husks and filled with various farming implements and the date "1833." The centre has a gilded name "William Farmer." It is a high-quality piece.
**Size:** 10.75" (27cm) tall.
**Marks:** Unmarked.

# Boy On A Ram Named & Dated Jug

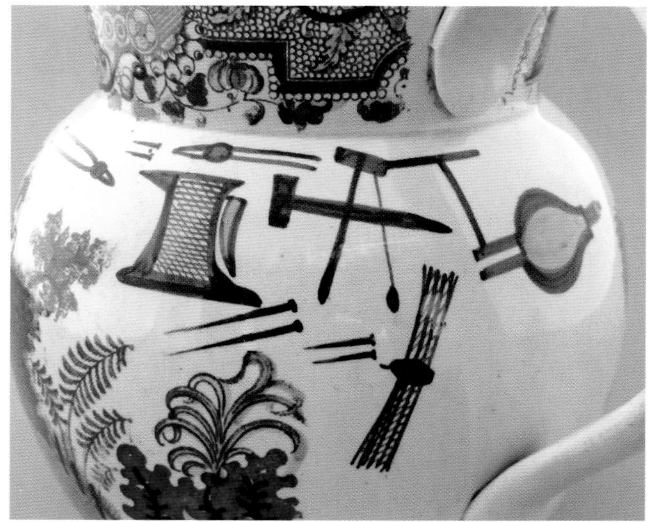

**Description:** An early named and dated chinoiserie pattern jug, c.1810, well printed with a wrap-around pattern called "Boy on a Ram" by an unknown maker. It shows a small boy sitting on a ram while leading another ram. They are following a boy with a parasol through a chinoiserie landscape that includes mountains, exotic plants and trees, and a castellated building. The pattern has been highlighted with enamels in a typical Pratt palette of green, orange, yellow, and brown. Below the spout, it has the painted name and date, "John Webster (spelt "Iohn Webfter'), 1810." It also has hand-painted tools around the jug that are probably blacksmith or farrier tools. They include an anvil, pliers, bellows, and nails.
**Size:** 7" (18cm) tall.
**Marks:** Unmarked.

# Chinoiserie Fern Named & Dated Jug

**Description:** A Swansea "Chinoiserie Fern" or "Fern Tree" pattern jug, c.1815, printed with a wrap-around chinoiserie pattern that has a large fern tree as its main feature. It has a blue printed name and date to the centre that reads "EVAN GRIFFITHS, ABERDARE, 1815." Evan Griffiths was a prominent and wealthy member of the Aberdare community. He was always linked to "Ty Mawr" (translated as "The Big House"), where he ran a large and thriving grocery business. Evan was a very important member of the Calvinistic Methodist community. "Ty Mawr" was knocked down in the 1970s.
**Size:** 6.5" (16.5cm) tall.
**Marks:** Blue printed blue-dot workman's mark.

# Lucano Jug

**Description:** A "Bridge of Lucano" pattern jug, c.1825. This pattern was possibly taken from a source engraved by George Hackert entitled "The Tomb of Plautius Lucanus" and represents The Bridge of Lucano near Tivoli to the East of Rome. The front of the jug has a panel that is painted with a crown and initials, "G. R. Mc." There is a painted implement at the bottom that possibly relates to the Saddlery trade.
**Size:** 5.5" (14cm) tall.
**Marks:** Unmarked.

# Named & Dated Frog Mug

**Description:** A fabulous named and dated frog mug, c.1829, printed with an "Indian Sporting" border and eight different animal prints. These were taken mainly from *A General History of Quadrupeds*, Thomas Bewick, 1790. The base of the mug is inscribed "James Swinn" and an indistinct address. It also has a printed "T. M. B." and "1829." Inside the mug, it has a very realistic and beautifully painted frog.

**Size:** 4" (10cm) tall.

**Marks:** Unmarked.

T.M.B
1829

# Initialled Mug

**Description:** A blue printed mug, c.1825, decorated with a stylised wrap-around scene of people fishing in a river beneath a bridge. There are large buildings either side and palm trees. It has a floral border around the rim on the outside and a semi-chinoiserie border to the inside. On the front of the mug, the potter has left a circular hole in the transfer that has been filled with a red-painted cartouche that reads "T.D. No. 8." Maybe this was from a set of ale mugs in a tavern that were all numbered differently?
**Size:** 5.25" (13cm) tall.
**Marks:** Unmarked.

# Swansea Italian Pattern Puzzle Jug

**Description:** A Swansea named and dated puzzle jug, c.1821, printed with the "Italian" pattern that was first introduced by Spode in about 1816. It has two borders, the standard "Italian" pattern border printed below the nozzles and a floral border printed above. Puzzle jugs were an amusement of the time. The drinker would have to work out how to extract the liquid content without spilling any. This could only be achieved by covering two of the nozzles and a secret hole under the handle and sucking on the remaining spout. This example is named and dated "S.E. TREVETHAN, 1821." This jug was probably made for Sampson Trevethan who was a mining engineer from Chacewater, Cornwall.
**Size:** 8.25" (21cm) tall.
**Marks:** Unmarked.

# Boy With A Whip Named & Dated Jug

**Description:** An early named and dated chinoiserie pattern jug, c.1814, printed with a pattern known as "Boy with a Whip," which was probably made in Swansea. The pattern shows a small boy with a whip talking to a man with a parasol. They are standing on the bank of a large lake or river and there is a large castellated building on an island in the background. The boy may actually be holding a fishing pole and not a whip. Under the spout, it has a hand painted name, place, and date that reads "JAMES BROWNIOHN, WOOD HOUSE FARM, 1814." Note how they have written the "J" in "BROWNJOHN" as an "I." Also note the handle, which is moulded to give the appearance of bamboo.

**Size:** 8" (20cm) tall.

**Marks:** Unmarked.

# Net Pattern Named & Dated Punch Bowl

**Description:** A large punch bowl, c.1807, printed with the "Net" pattern consisting of four chinoiserie cartouches amongst a stylised floral background. The middle of the pattern usually has a floral centre set on what looks like a net background, hence the name "Net" pattern. It was used for serving punch, a drink consisting of various alcoholic and fruit parts that owes its origins to an Indian drink. This example is beautifully painted with "Ann Sayers, Southgate, Middlesex, 1807." The bowl has a red-brown colour around the rim that matches the colour of the script to the centre.
**Size:** 13.75" (35cm) in diameter, 6" (15cm) tall.
**Marks:** Unmarked.

# Initialled Spirit Barrel

**Description:** An initialled spirit barrel, c.1825, printed with a view of "Osterley Park, Middlesex" and was possibly made by Ridgway. It shows a scene of deer in a landscape before a very distinctive arched bridge. There are people walking across the bridge and people fishing from a boat, and Osterley Park house is in the background. Spirit barrels were for storing and carrying a variety of spirits. This example is initialled "A.R.," which were presumably the initials of the original owner.

**Size:** 4.25" (11cm) tall.

**Marks:** Unmarked.

# Laughing Dog Pattern Named & Dated Inkwell

**Description:** A superb "Chinese Family" pattern inkwell, c.1808. This is also known as the "Laughing Dog" pattern, as there is a dog in the foreground that looks as if it is chuckling. The inkwell has four holes around the outside to store quills and a central funnel which allows access to the ink. The underside of the inkwell was inscribed in the wet clay; it is almost impossible to read except for the date "1808." A name and place probably precedes the date.

**Size:** 3" (7.5cm) wide, 3" (7.5cm) tall.

**Marks:** Faintly inscribed to base.

# Conversation Pattern Loving Cup

**Description:** A striking loving cup, c.1790, printed in a very dark shade of blue with the "Conversation" pattern. This pattern is made up of typical chinoiserie elements being pagodas, islands, trees and a bridge. However, in this pattern, there are two figures standing on the bridge having a conversation, hence the title. The border, rim, and foot are decorated with yellow enamel, a colour that works extremely well with the dark blue to produce a very stunning object. On the front of the cup, there is a hand painted panel that reads "I Worrall, 1790." The "I" in this case was probably meant to be a "J," as they wrote "Js" as "Is" in those days. This is a very early date and was right near the start of the transferware inception.

**Size:** 5.25" (13cm) tall, 7.5" (19cm) handle to handle.

**Marks:** Unmarked.

# Initialled Frog Mug

**Description:** An "Ornate Pagodas" pattern frog mug with initialled panel, c.1815, printed with a wrap-around chinoiserie pattern that has a landscape of pagodas and a castle. There are figures on a bridge in the foreground. This example has a hand painted monogram of "BAH" to the centre and an extremely realistic frog inside. These frog mugs were designed as novelty and fun pieces. The idea was not to tell the drinker that there was a frog inside and they would get a terrible fright when they emptied the mug! Note the fake screw heads that can be seen "holding" the handle to the body.
**Size:** 5" (12.5cm) tall.
**Marks:** Unmarked.

# Rural Christening Mug

**Description:** A rural scene christening mug, c.1824, printed with a scene of figures in a rural landscape before a large building. There is a man fishing in the river to the left-hand side of the print. The mug is decorated in hand painted script with "Martha Turton, Born 14 June 1824." Unusually, it has a single flower from the border pattern printed to the underside.

**Size:** 3.25" (8cm) tall.

**Marks:** Blue printed flower from border.

# Fig Tree Pattern Named & Dated Jug

**Description:** A named and dated chinoiserie pattern jug, c.1804, printed with a pattern known as the "Fig Tree." This pattern has a chinoiserie landscape that includes pagodas, boats on a river, birds, fences, and a bridge. It has a large fig tree as its main feature, hence the title for this pattern. Underneath the spout, there is a hand painted shield that reads "Samuel Sanders, Durfley, Gloucestershire, 1804." Note how the painter has abbreviated the name "Samuel" to fit into the space available and the use of an "f" instead of an "s" in the middle of the place name "Dursley." Dursley is a small market town in Gloucestershire situated between Gloucester and Bristol.

**Size:** 8" (20cm) tall.

**Marks:** Unmarked.

# Broseley Pattern Loving Cup

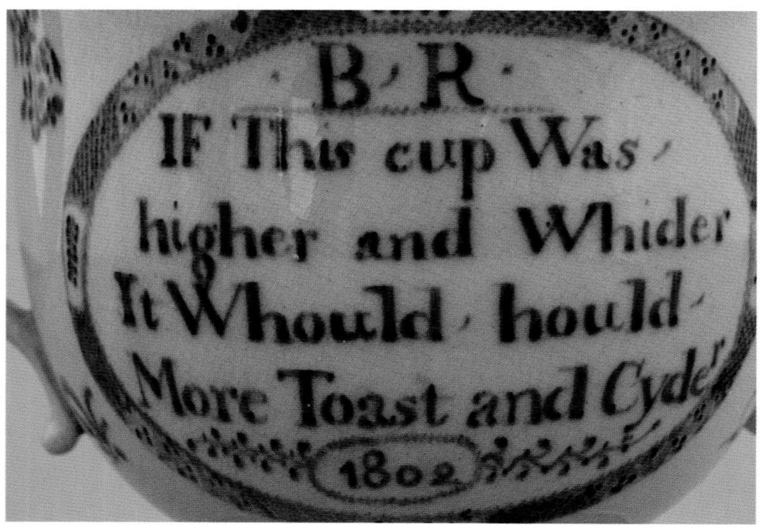

**Description:** A blue printed loving cup, c.1802, decorated with the "Broseley" pattern to one side and has an amusing rhyme to the other. It also has the initials "BR" and the date "1802" within the central panel. The panel's verse reads "IF This cup Was higher and Whider / It Whould hould / More Toast and Cyder." Note the old English spelling of the words "wider," "would," "hold," and "cider."
**Size:** 6.5" (16.5cm) tall, 9.25" (23.5cm) handle to handle.
**Marks:** Unmarked.

# WILLOW PATTERN INITIALLED & DATED JUG

**Description:** An initialled and dated jug, c.1802, well printed with the standard "Willow" pattern, which is one of the most widely produced patterns within the field of transferware. This jug is a very elegant shape standing on a pedestal foot. Beneath the spout it has the initials and date, "IC, 1802." It is such a shame that in most cases we will never know the real history behind these named and dated wares. It was obviously very significant to "IC" at the time (or "JC').
**Size:** 8.75" (22.5cm) tall.
**Marks:** Unmarked.

# Swansea Named & Dated Jug

**Description:** A Swansea "Chinoiserie Fern" or "Fern Tree" pattern jug, c.1805, printed with a wrap-around chinoiserie pattern that has a large and prominent fern as its main feature. Under the spout, it has the name and date, "Matthew & Hannah Tym, 1805." It has an ochre edge to the rim and handle terminals. Note the beautiful moulding to the handle in the form of acanthus leaves.

**Size:** 8.25" (21cm) tall.

**Marks:** Unmarked.

# Chinaman With Rocket Named & Dated Jug

**Description:** A chinoiserie named and dated jug, c.1800, printed with a pattern called "Chinaman with Rocket." It is decorated with two identical prints of a Chinese landscape, one to each side. There is a bridge at the centre with a man travelling across. It looks rather like the man is holding a rocket. Beneath the spout, there is the name and date, "James Taylor, Heywood, 1800." Heywood is a small town situated north of Manchester in Lancashire.
**Size:** 8.5" (21.5cm) tall.
**Marks:** Unmarked.

# Named & Dated Punch Bowl

**Description:** A named and dated punch bowl, c.1800. It has blue-printed chinoiserie island scenes decorating both the interior and exterior. The border is a typical chinoiserie design, but has the unusual feature of cartouches with pairs of sailing vessels in them. The interior of the bowl is hand painted with "One, Bowl, More, And, Then, Thomas, And, Mary, Turner, 1800." You will notice that each word in the inscription is separated with a comma. There was a notable decorator at the Swansea factory of this period who used commas to separate words and therefore this bowl is attributed to Swansea.
**Size:** 12.25" (31cm) in diameter.
**Marks:** Unmarked.

# Named & Dated Jug

**Description:** A named and dated chinoiserie pattern jug, c.1797, printed with a pattern called "Fisherman with Trap," which has a wide chinoiserie landscape with a fisherman holding a trap on the end of a pole. There are two borders on this jug. The first is a stylized chinoiserie-type with flowers and scrolls around the shoulder of the jug. The second is a geometric border around the rim. Underneath the spout, it has the name and date, "James Taylor, 1797." There are various floral sprays around the inscription and the collar of the jug. Note the very unusual and elegant handle.

**Size:** 8.25" (21cm) tall.

**Marks:** Unmarked.

# Lucano Spirit Barrel

**Description:** A "Lucano" pattern initialled and dated spirit barrel, c.1821. This pattern was possibly taken from a source engraved by George Hackert entitled "The Tomb of Plautius Lucanus" and represents The Bridge of Lucano near Tivoli to the East of Rome. The front of the barrel has a blue painted mark that reads, "CB, 1821." Spirit barrels were for holding, transporting and dispensing a wide range of spirits.
**Size:** 5" (12.5cm) tall, 4" (10cm) in diameter.
**Marks:** Unmarked.

# Spode Filigree Child's Teapot

**Description:** A Spode "Filigree" pattern child's teapot, c.1825, printed with a floral design that has a basket of flowers as its main feature. One side of the teapot has a blue printed panel and initials that read "EJ." This was done by Spode at the time of manufacture, as you can see the cut-out in the transfer left for the initials and the fact that they are printed and under-glazed. Spode is not particularly known for doing this type of special order ware and examples are rare.

**Size:** 6" (15cm) long.

**Marks:** Blue printed SPODE.

# Named & Dated Money Box

**Description:** A "Broseley" pattern named and dated money box, c.1836, hand-painted with a panel that reads "Benjamin Hemsworth, 1836." It has a slot above this panel into which coins are inserted. Money boxes do not survive in great numbers, as often the only way to extract the coins was to break the pottery open.
**Size:** 4.5" (11.5cm) tall.
**Marks:** Unmarked.

# Pagoda & Palms Guglet

**Description:** A chinoiserie initialled and dated guglet, c.1806, printed with the "Pagoda and Palms" pattern. This is a scene of two figures in conversation in a Chinese landscape that includes several palm trees and pagodas, hence the name. It has a red painted rim and the initials "MJ" painted on the body. On the underside of the vessel, it has the date "1806" painted. A guglet is a long-necked vessel used to store water before it was served at a dinner table. The name is of Anglo-Indian origin, but is also thought to be a description of the sound the water makes when it is poured as it glugs out. It could also possibly have been a decanter for wine.
**Size:** 7.25" (18.5cm) tall, 5.25" (13cm) diameter at base.
**Marks:** Unmarked.

# West Auckland Market Plate

**Description:** A blue printed plate, c.1836, decorated with "SUCCESS TO THE WEST AUCKLAND MARKET, OPENED 17 SEP.. 1836." This plate was probably produced in the North-East of England to promote and raise awareness of the newly opened market. West Auckland is a town in County Durham, in northeast England. After the opening of the Stockton and Darlington railway in 1825, the search for coal escalated dramatically in the West Auckland area. The population increased as a consequence of the resulting promise of employment. West Auckland began to expand and flourish. Plates such as these were almost certainly produced in small quantities and are therefore uncommon.

**Size:** 9.75" (25cm) in diameter.

**Marks:** Impressed star mark.

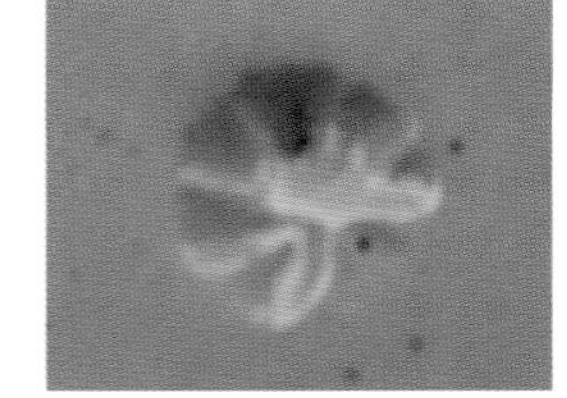

# Lakin Prince of Wales Armorial Soup Dish

**Description:** A Thomas Lakin soup dish, c.1815, printed with a stunning armorial. It consists of the Prince of Wales feathers, a lion on a coronet and the border is made up of the Union flowers; rose, thistle, and shamrock. This service is reputed to have been ordered by George IV when he was the Prince Regent for use in Brighton Pavilion and was subsequently passed down to be part of the collection of Queen Mary.
**Size:** 9.75" (25cm) in diameter.
**Marks:** Unmarked.

# Spode Tiber Coffee House Plate

**Description:** A Spode plate, c.1820, printed with the "Tiber" pattern, although the Spode factory name was "Rome." This pattern is made up of an out-of-place "Column of Trajan" and the "Ponte St. Angelo" on the river Tiber which makes up the rest of the pattern. Both elements were taken from a published work *Views of Rome and its Vicinity*, J. Merigot and R. Edwards, 1796-98. The back is printed with "HARRISONS, NEW HUMMUMS COFFEE HOUSE." This plate was a special order by Mr. Harrison to use in his hotel and coffee house in Convent Garden, London. Coffee houses were an important part of the social, political, and commercial life at this time. In the early nineteenth century, some of the more up-market houses expanded and became more like restaurants and hotels. They ordered their own high-quality china, often having their own names marked on pieces. This particular coffee house was demolished in 1888.

**Size:** 9.75" (25cm) in diameter.

**Marks:** Impressed Spode.

# Tee Total Plate

**Description:** A "Tee Total" plate, c.1835, printed with three chinoiserie cartouches and a central panel that reads "TeeTotal." This plate was produced to show that the owner was a teetotaller, though it is not known whether it was actually used or just displayed to advertise the owner's beliefs. Teetotalism is said to have come from the Temperance Society in the early nineteenth century and refers to either the practice of, or the promotion of, completely abstaining from alcohol. This is usually undertaken for religious, philosophical, family, or health reasons.
**Size:** 7.5" (19cm) in diameter.
**Marks:** Unmarked.

# Spode Hatchetts Platter

**Description:** A Spode platter, c.1825, printed on the outside of the platter with the "Jasmine" pattern border print. The centre has a very finely engraved and detailed print. It depicts "Hatchetts," The White Horse Cellar in Piccadilly, London. Hatchetts is said to have been a coffee house and hotel that was also a coaching terminal for the westbound traffic. This building is now the Ritz Hotel. Bailey & Thomas may have been a coaching company that used this destination or the company running the coffee house at this time.
**Size:** 15" (38cm) wide.
**Marks:** Green printed SPODE.

# Chinoiserie Jug With Ship

**Description:** A chinoiserie pattern jug, c.1810, well printed with an unknown scene of all the usual chinoiserie aspects, the pagodas, the bridge, the trees, and the islands. It has a wide border with several moths or butterflies. Underneath the spout, there is a beautifully engraved transfer of a ship. This has been let into the chinoiserie pattern and is of high quality. The three-masted vessel appears to be flying a British flag. This may represent a clipper ship from a trading company and the jug could have been a special order piece for it.

**Size:** 8.25" (21cm) tall.

**Marks:** Unmarked.

# Minton Tavern Plate

**Description:** A Minton tavern plate, c.1835, printed on the outer rim with Minton's "Arabesque" pattern border print. The centre is printed with a riverside tavern called the "ARTICHOKE TAVERN, BLACKWALL." This was a wooden-built tavern on the north bank of the River Thames, London. This plate was obviously specially commissioned by the owners of the tavern for use on their premises. The tavern was knocked down in 1889 to make way for the Blackwall Tunnel, which was being constructed at that time.

**Size:** 9" (23cm) in diameter.

**Marks:** Impressed Improved Stone China.

# Chinoiserie Wheat Sheaf Bowl

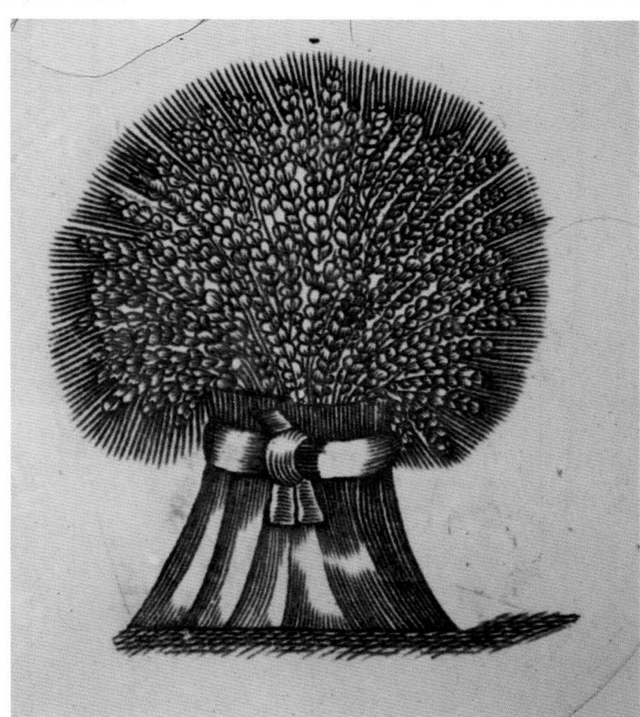

**Description:** A chinoiserie pattern bowl, c.1800, printed to the outside with a scene of two figures in conversation on a bridge with an island in the background. This is a very typical chinoiserie scene for the time. The centre of the bowl is printed with a beautifully engraved wheat sheaf. A wheat sheaf was a very important symbol of prosperity and well-being. It showed that the ever-important and critical harvest had been a success. A successful harvest in those days was a matter of life and death.
**Size:** 8.75" (22cm) in diameter, 3.5" (9cm) tall.
**Marks:** Unmarked.

# Spode India Plate

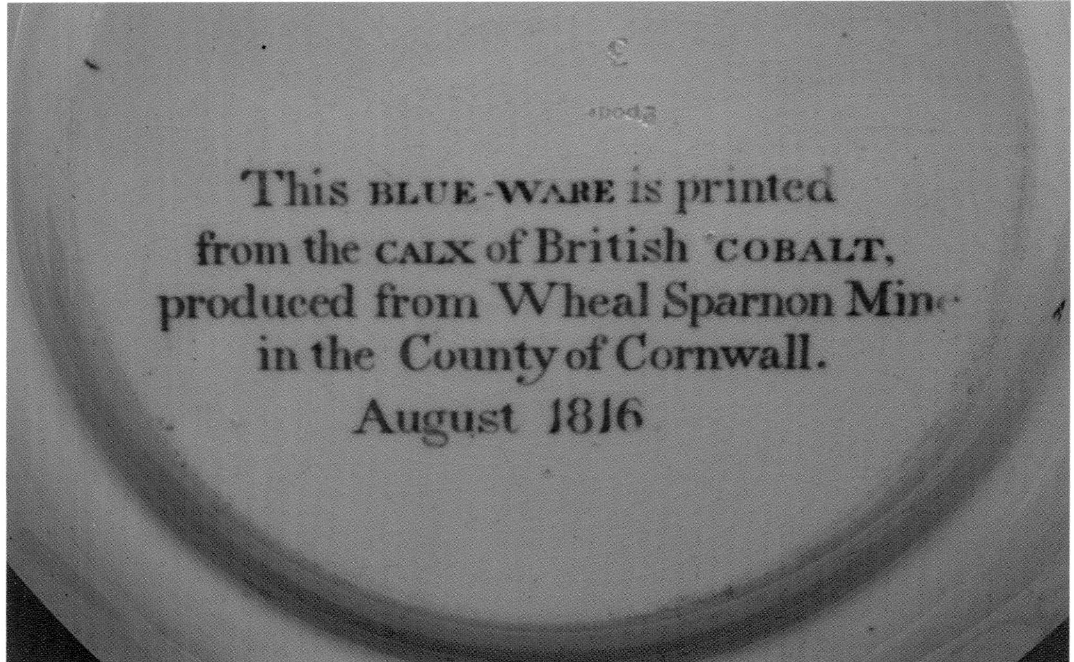


**Description:** A Spode "India" pattern plate, c.1816, printed with a design of a butterfly flying around a group of mixed flowers and is a copy of a Chinese original. The most important thing about this particular plate is the blue-printed mark to the reverse. It reads "This BLUE-WARE is printed from the CALX of British COBALT produced from Wheal Sparnon Mine in the County of Cornwall. August 1816." The word "Wheal" means mine in Cornish and was omitted after a short production run when they realised they were actually writing "mine Sparnon mine." See the next piece for the non-Wheal version that succeeded it. This mark was a patriotic slogan that basically said "Buy British."

**Size:** 9.75" (25cm) in diameter.

**Marks:** Impressed Spode.

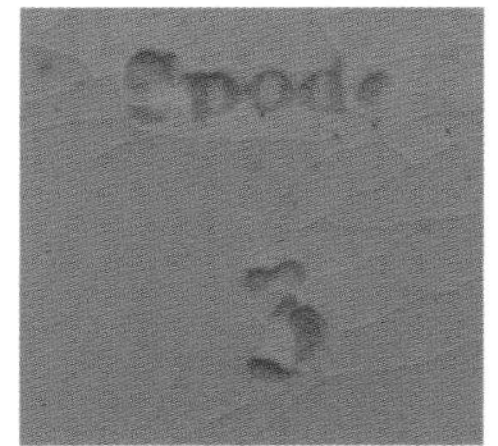

# Spode Italian Well & Tree Platter

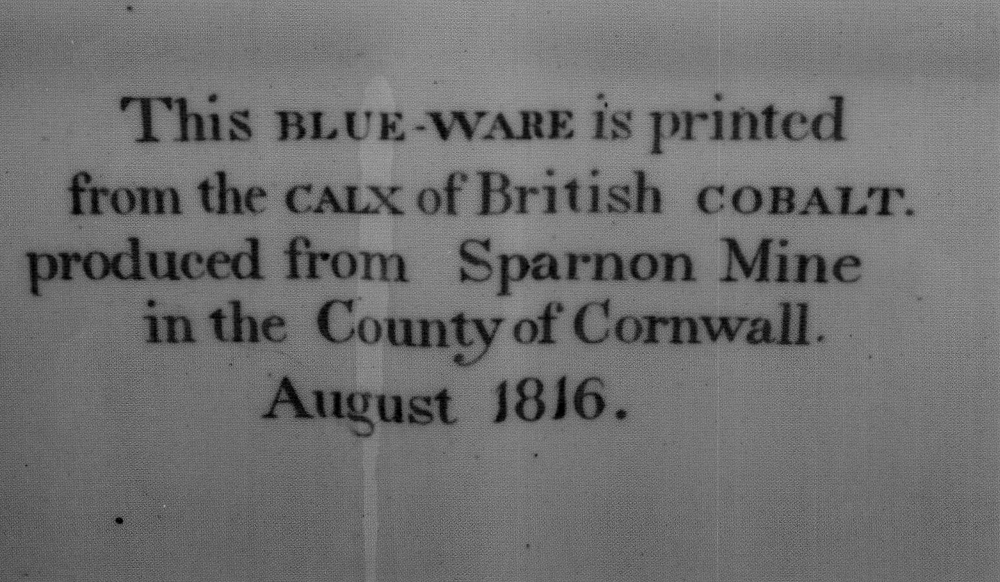

**Description:** A Spode "Italian" pattern well and tree platter, c.1816. This scene was copied from a pastoral landscape painted by Claude Lorraine in 1638. This pattern is one of the most famous patterns in transferware. The most interesting thing about this particular example is the mark to the reverse. It reads "This BLUE-WARE is printed from the CALX of British COBALT. produced from Sparnon Mine in the County of Cornwall. August 1816." This later version has the word "Wheal" omitted from the mark. The object of this print was to promote the sale and purchase of British-made items.
**Size:** 20.75" (52.5cm) wide.
**Marks:** Impressed Spode.

# Broseley Bowl

**Description:** A very unusual religious bowl, c.1815, printed to the interior and exterior rim with a large print of the "Broseley" pattern border. The centre is printed with a very detailed engraving titled "CHRIST'S Ascension into HEAVEN." It shows Christ in the clouds flanked by two angels. If we consider that the general population of the time was extremely religious, why are items such as this so uncommon?

**Size:** 7.75" (19.5cm) in diameter, 3" (7.5cm) tall.

**Marks:** Unmarked.

# Spode Gun Room Plate

**Description:** A very interesting Spode plate, c.1815, printed with the Union border found on the Spode "Union Wreath" pattern, but with an edge stringing added. The centre has a print of the Prince of Wales feathers and the words "GUN ROOM." The plate must have been part of a special order placed with Spode by the Prince of Wales (George IV to be). It was part of a bigger service that was to be used in a gun room on one of the Royal shooting estates. Gun rooms were where the shooting party would gather before and after a shoot to socialize and make merry. An interesting thing about this pattern is that the border was probably designed for this service and then used by Spode as part of another pattern, "Union Wreath," ten years later.

**Size:** 8.25" (21cm) in diameter.

**Marks:** Impressed and printed SPODE.

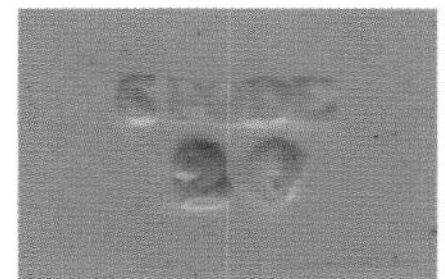

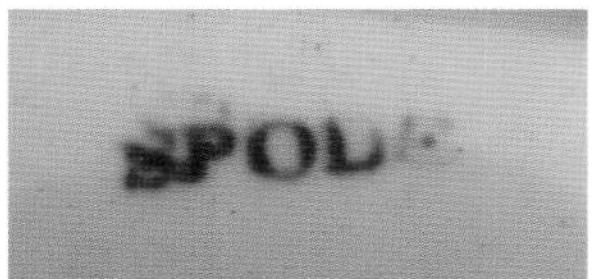

# Arms of Newcastle Plate & Soup Dish

**Description:** Two early armorial pieces: an unknown maker soup dish, c.1800, and a Spode plate, c.1815. The soup dish is printed to the rim with a chinoiserie border print and has the Arms of Newcastle on the centre, c.1800. The plate is Spode and is printed partly with a pattern from the "Greek" series, c.1815. It has the panels and vases from the "Zeus in his Chariot" print. The central "Zeus" scene has been replaced on this example by a finely engraved armorial of the Arms of Newcastle. In both cases the armorials read "Fortiter Defendit Triumphans," which means "Bravely Defends and Triumphs." These words originate from the English Civil War when Newcastle was attacked for three months by Cromwell's Parliamentarians supporting Scottish allies in 1644. Both of these examples were possibly ordered to be used in an official building within Newcastle, but were manufactured about fifteen years apart. Perhaps pieces from the original service were broken and a new service was ordered from a different potter later on.

**Size:** Both 9.25" (23.5cm) in diameter.

**Marks:** Soup dish unmarked, plate printed SPODE.

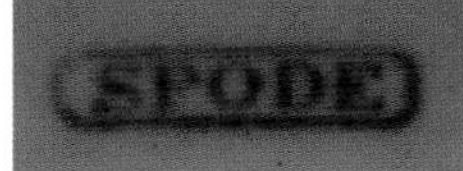

# British Temperance League Plate

**Description:** A "British Temperance League" plate, c.1837. This plate has a floral border and an illustrative armorial to the centre. It reads "FIRM AS AN OAK, SOBRIETY, DOMESTIC COMFORT, BE THOU FAITHFUL UNTO DEATH." There are symbols on the shield at the centre that mean industry, freedom, plenty, health, wealth, wisdom, death, religion, and eternity. Below this, there are empty and discarded drinking vessels which illustrate teetotalism. This was one of the main philosophies followed by the Temperance League. This plate was probably not meant to be used, but to act as a symbol that the owner was a supporter or member of the Temperance League.

**Size:** 8" (20cm) in diameter.

**Marks:** Impressed 0.

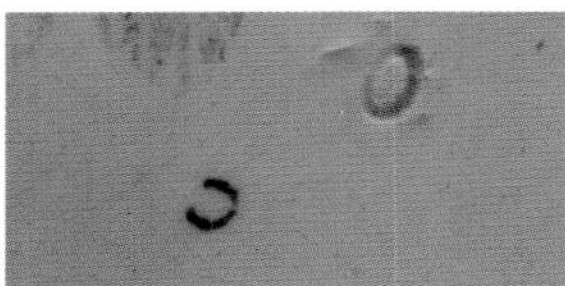

# Spode Tile

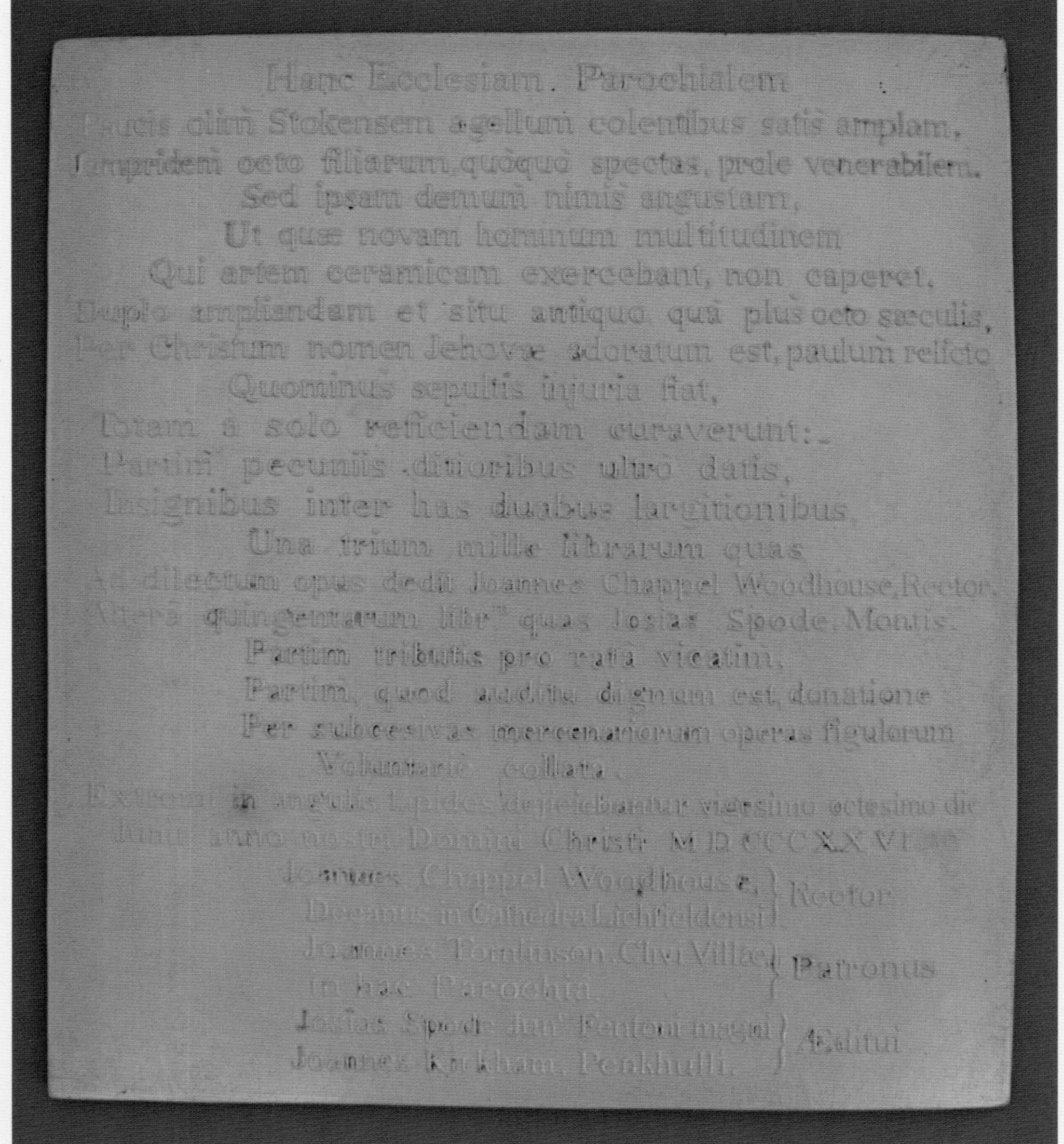


**Description:** This extraordinary Spode tile was made in connection with the building of a new church in Stoke-upon-Trent in 1826, which was to be large enough to accommodate 1672 people. Spode made five tiles, each in a different body, to be laid in the corner stones of the Stoke New Church during construction. The tiles were a "Best Porcelain" tile with a painting of Stoke Old Church, a "Rich Brown" porcelain tile, a "Jasper" tile, a "Patent Stone Porcelain," and finally, one of "The Best Blue printed Pottery." They were laid by the Very Rev. Dean of Litchfield, John Tomlinson, Esq., Mr. Kirkham, and Josiah Spode, Esq. (two tiles) on 28 June 1826. All five tiles were superb examples of Spode's work and had a Latin inscription, in relief, on their backs. The English translation reads "This Parish Church, at first well adapted to the few scattered Husbandmen, who, in early times, composed the Inhabitants of Stoke-upon-Trent, having given birth to Eight other sacred Edifices, but at length become inadequate to contain within her Walls, the New Population, which the Local Manufacture, The Potters' Art, had gathered around her; was rebuilt from the foundations, on an extended scale, as near to the Spot, where for more than Eight Centuries, Worship to God, in Christ's Name, had been

paid, as a regard to the Ashes of the Dead would allow, by means of Resources, supplied; -partly, by the Voluntary Offerings of the Opulent, and among these most conspicuous a Gift of £3,000 from John Chappel Woodhouse, Rector and of £500 from Josiah Spode, of the Mount; partly by a Parochial Rare; and lastly yet most worthy of record, by Contributions arising from the supernumerary Labours of the Working Classes spontaneously bestowed. The Corner Stones of the Foundations were laid the 28th of June, in the Year of Our Lord Christ, 1826." The blue printed tile was laid by Mr. Kirkham in the North West corner of the church's foundations. The church still stands today and these tiles are not visible, so they were presumably encased in stone and mortar. This brings us to the question of the existence of this example and a similar tile in one of the other bodies still in the care of the Spode museum. Did Spode make a single spare of each tile in case something happened to the tile before or during the time when it was being laid in the church? The most feasible suggestion is that there were two made of each tile and one was laid in the church and the other was given as a memento to the person who laid the tile, in this case, Mr. Kirkham. The pattern on this example was specially engraved for the tile as illustrated by the fact that the pattern has no cuts or breaks in the transfer. This pattern was never used again by Spode. The church was completed in August 1829; sadly Josiah Spode II died in July, 1827 so he never saw the completed building. All of the information above is recorded in a published work, *History of the Staffordshire Potteries,* by Simeon Shaw, 1829. The information can be regarded as correct because the work is contemporary to the information it describes.

**Size:** 13.75 (35cm) x 11.75 (30cm).

**Marks:** Impressed SPODE to the face.

# Spode Armorial Plate

**Description:** A Spode armorial plate, c.1820, printed with the border and inner motifs from the "Trophies Dagger" or "Fitzhugh" pattern. The pattern was copied from a Chinese service brought back by the Fitzhugh family, who were very active in the East India Trading company in the late 18th century. This is, therefore, where the pattern gets its name. The four panels in the pattern are treasures or accomplishments and represent music, chess, calligraphy, and painting. The centre of this example has a hand-painted armorial, but no details are known about who commissioned it or owned it. It is printed on a heavy, stone china body.

**Size:** 9.75" (25cm) in diameter.

**Marks:** Impressed SPODE'S NEW STONE.

# Spode Armorial Plate

**Description:** A Spode armorial plate, c.1825, printed to the outer edge with the border print from the "Geranium" pattern. The centre is printed with an armorial that reads "BENINGNO NUMINE," which translates as "By the Favour of the Heavens" or "By Divine Providence." These were the arms for William Copeland III, who was the majority shareholder in Spode at this time. There was another service, commissioned when William Copeland married Sarah Yates in 1826, that had this armorial combined with that of the Yates family.

**Size:** 9.75" (25cm) in diameter.

**Marks:** Blue printed SPODE.

# Spode Armorial Sauce Boat

**Description:** A Spode armorial sauce boat, c.1825, printed with the border print from the "Geranium" pattern and the arms of the Skinners Company on each side. It reads "TO GOD ONLY BE ALL GLORY" beneath the arms. This was a specially commissioned service by the Worshipful Company of Skinners of the City of London. This pattern with the Skinners' armorial design was ordered in the Spode period (seen here), during the Copeland and Garrett period, and the Copeland period, well into the twentieth century, presumably because of breakages and/or growing membership.

**Size:** 8" (20cm) long.

**Marks:** Blue printed SPODE.

# Spode Armorial Sauce Tureen Stand

**Description:** A Spode armorial circular sauce tureen stand, c.1825, printed with the border print from the "Jasmine" pattern and a central armorial of bees around a beehive. This armorial was produced for St. John's College and a beehive usually stands for industry. There have been many St. John's Colleges, but it is not clear for which this service was made.
**Size:** 7.5" (19cm) in diameter.
**Marks:** Blue printed SPODE.

# Spode Armorial Plate

**Description:** A Spode armorial plate, c.1815, printed with a geometric border that seems to have been designed especially for this service. The centre has the arms of Earl Ferrers printed in blue and reads "MALGRE L' ENVIE" on a banner. This translates as "In Spite of Envy." These arms are in two parts and the Spode designers have put the other element within the border at the 12 o'clock position. It is printed on a heavy, stone china body.

**Size:** 9.75" (25cm) in diameter.

**Marks:** Blue printed Spode Stone China.

# Thompson Presentation Plate

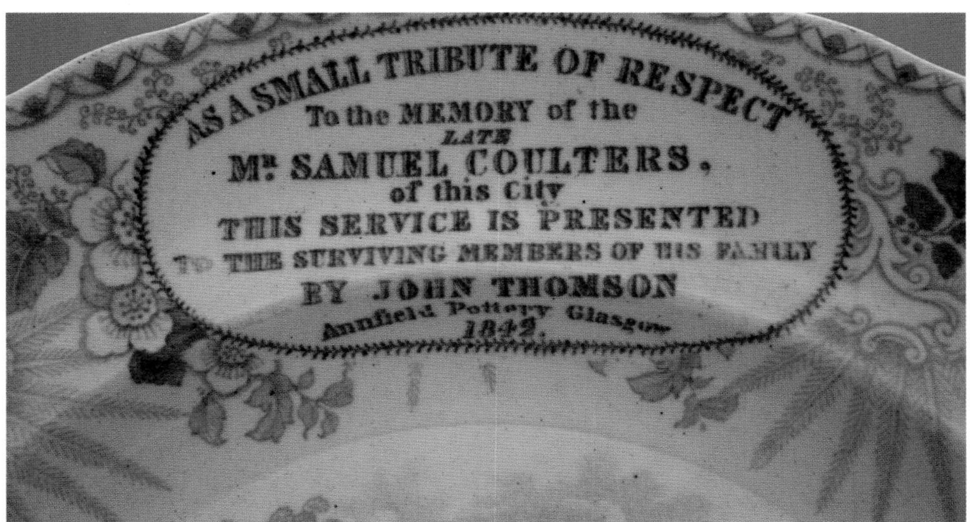


**Description:** A John Thompson plate, c.1842, printed with a romantic rural, probably European, scene of a farmer with three cows and a goat before a mountainous landscape. The border is made up of flowers, scrolls and radiating fronds. At the top of the plate, in the border, there is a touching inscription that reads "AS A SMALL TRIBUTE OF RESPECT, To the MEMORY of the LATE Mr. SAMUEL COULTERS of this city, THIS SERVICE IS PRESENTED TO THE SURVIVING MEMBERS OF HIS FAMILY BY JOHN THOMPSON, Annfield Pottery Glasgow, 1842." It is also printed with the Prince of Wales feathers on the reverse.

**Size:** 9" (23cm) in diameter.

**Marks:** Blue printed Prince of Wales.

# Eyre Tavern Soup Dishes

**Description:** A "Gamekeeper" pattern soup dish and a "Wild Rose" or "Nuneham Courtenay" soup dish, both, c.1825. The "Gamekeeper" pattern was taken from the published work *Rural Sports,* by Rev. W. B. Daniel, 1812. The original print does not include the building in the central background. This is Goodwood House, Sussex and was added to the design by the potter's engraver. The title mark is printed on a belt or possibly a dog collar. The view of "Nuneham Courtenay, Oxfordshire" was taken from an engraving by W. Cooke, published 1 February 1811. The view depicts Nuneham Park House on the left, which was the seat of Earl Harcourt. In the border at the top of both dishes is a printed mark for "EYRE TAVERN, ST. JOHN'S WOOD." These were special order services made for use in the Eyre Arms Tavern, Finchley Road, St. John's Wood, London. This tavern was later a hotel and was very close to Lord's cricket ground. As the "Eyre Tavern" print is the same in both cases, we can surmise that they were made by the same potter, which would link these two patterns.

**Size:** Both 10" (25.5cm) in diameter.

**Marks:** Blue printed Gamekeeper title mark. Wild Rose unmarked.

GAME KEEPER

# Brameld Boys Fishing Mug

**Description:** A Brameld "Boys Fishing" pattern large mug, c.1825, well printed with the famous scene of two boys fishing above a weir while their mother and sibling look on. It has a black printed tavern name of the "ROSE & CROWN BECKLEY." This was obviously ordered by the tavern from the factory, as they have left a rectangular hole in the transfer for the name to be written. The Rose & Crown Tavern is in Beckley, Rye, East Sussex, and remains there today.

**Size:** 6.5" (16.5cm) tall.

**Marks:** Unmarked.

# Trial / Apprentice Mug

**Description:** A blue printed trial or apprentice mug, c.1825, printed with a small section of a larger design that is repeated eleven times around the circumference of this mug. Training and practicing were hugely important parts of the transfer printing process. The interesting thing is that these were obviously made, but were not intended for sale. Did they only survive because the apprentice was allowed to keep the trial pieces he made?

**Size:** 3.75" (9.5cm) tall.

**Marks:** Unmarked.

# Kings Arms Dish

**Description:** A "Pagoda and Palms Variation" large serving bowl, c.1815, printed with a chinioserie pattern that includes pagodas, islands, and boats. It has a very distinctive couple in the foreground that look to be in deep conversation; "Gossiping Women" is indeed another title for this pattern. At the centre, it has a blue printed panel that reads "KING'S ARMS, PALACE YARD." This relates to a tavern in Westminster, London, that was also a hotel. It was a meeting place for Freemasons from as early as 1771. Because of its location in Westminster, many official government meetings and hearings took place there, including a delegation during the woollen industry dispute in 1819. *Public Houses, Publicans and Public House Addresses, Pigot, 1839*, lists the proprietor as Eliza Ann Brown. Although this dish predates this reference by some twenty-five years, it is not inconceivable that she was at the tavern at the same time as this dish.

**Size:** 16.75" (42.5cm) in diameter.

**Marks:** Unmarked.

Chapter 7

# Miscellaneous Wares

**This chapter has all of the items of pottery that simply do not fit into any other chapter. This includes utilitarian pieces, items made for display, items used in horticulture, and those used in recreation.**

# Spode Caramanian Series Garden Seat

**Description:** A Spode "Caramanian" series garden seat, c.1810. The sides are printed with two panels of "A Triumphal Arch of Tripoli in Barbary" and the top of the seat is printed with a view of "Antique Fragments at Limisso." The Spode engravers used a source from a published work entitled *Views in the Ottoman Empire* by Luigi Mayer, c.1803. The remaining areas of the seat are printed with the "Caramanian" sheet pattern that is more normally found on handles. Garden seats were copied from Chinese originals. They were made for use outside or in conservatories and, as such, not many survive.

**Size:** 18.75" (47.5cm) tall.

**Marks:** Impressed SPODE to the underside.

# Grazing Rabbits Vases

**Description:** A superb pair of "Grazing Rabbits" pattern vases and covers, c.1815, each printed with this famous pattern of rabbits in a country landscape. The vases have moulded knops in the form of a woman and child. The vase shape is in the style of earlier Chinese examples. They were possibly used for storage, but more likely were just for display. If this is the case, then this makes them extremely rare within transferware, as 99.99% of all items were utilitarian and were designed to be used.
**Size:** 9" (23cm) tall.
**Marks:** Unmarked.

# Potpourri & Cover

**Description:** A "Boy on a Buffalo" pattern potpourri, c.1810, well printed with a scene of a boy riding a buffalo; possibly made by Spode. It has a removable lid which has ten holes around the outside and a central hole. This could either have been used to display floral specimens or for potpourri.
**Size:** 7.5" (19cm) tall, 4.25" (11cm) wide.
**Marks:** Blue painted workman's mark.

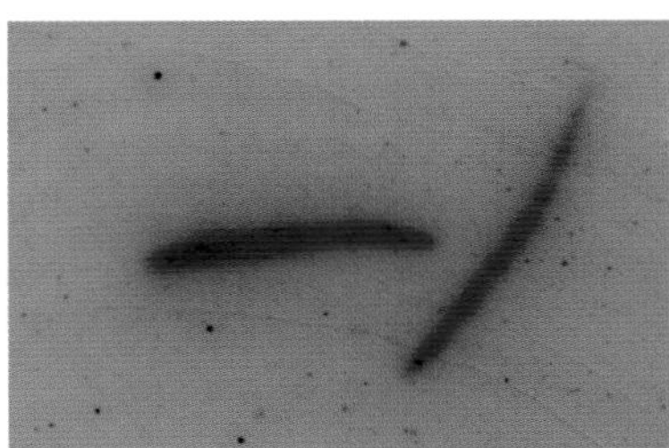

# Audley End Flask

**Description:** A bottle-shaped flask, c.1825, printed to both sides with part of a view of "Audley End, Essex" by an unknown maker. Note the unusual use of a reflection in the lake of the large house. Flasks were used for storing and transporting a wide variety of liquids, but primarily spirits.
**Size:** 5.25" (13cm) tall, 2.75 (7cm) wide.
**Marks:** Unmarked.

# Copeland & Garrett Sander

**Description:** A Copeland & Garrett, Late Spode sander, c.1835, printed with a pattern known as "Basket, Brick & Vase" which is usually associated with Adams, Clews, or Minton. This sander was an essential part of a writing or desk set. In the days when quills and inks were used for writing, a sander would sprinkle sand or fine powder onto the wet ink to prevent smudging.

**Size:** 2.25" (6cm) tall, 2" (5cm) in diameter.

**Marks:** Blue printed C & G, Late Spode.

# Temple Pattern Money Box

**Description:** A "Temple" pattern money box by an unknown maker, c.1815. This pattern was copied from an original Chinese design by many potters. Money boxes are fairly uncommon items, because, with most designs, the only way to extract the money successfully was to break the pottery open. Note how the slot to insert the money is quite long. This was because some of the coins at the time had a much larger diameter than today's coins. Note also the typical Georgian design feature of an acorn-shaped knop.

**Size:** 5.25" (13cm) tall, 3" (7.5cm) in diameter.

**Marks:** Unmarked.

# Two Figures Pattern Vessel

**Description:** A most unusual vessel, c.1810, printed with the "Two Figures" pattern. This pattern was taken from a Chinese export design and has two figures in front of a pagoda or temple. This object is most unusual and has a variety of possible uses. It has been suggested that it was an early form of a stirrup cup that was passed around before the huntsmen set off on the hunt. It could also have been a master salt that would have sat in the middle of a table. The shape of the item almost certainly copies a Chinese form, possibly that of a Chinese lady's foot. Foot binding was a custom practiced on young girls and women for approximately one thousand years in China, beginning in the 10th century. As this object's use is largely uncertain, it is listed here in the "Miscellaneous" section.
**Size:** 5.5" (14cm) long, 2.5" (6.5cm) tall.
**Marks:** Unmarked.

# Garniture of CJ Mason Pots & Covers

**Description:** A garniture or set of three pots and covers, c.1825. They were made by C. J. Mason, Fenton Works, Lane Delph, Staffordshire. They are well printed with a wrap-around scene of "Trentham Hall, Staffordshire." This pattern is also known as "Hercules Fountain." The pattern has two deer in the foreground and an enormous fountain before the house. These pots were probably small storage jars, which are relatively uncommon in transferware.

**Size:** Large 4.25" (11cm) tall, small 3.5" (8.5cm) tall.

**Marks:** Blue printed SEMI-CHINA WARRANTED.

# SPODE TOWER PATTERN CHAMBER CANDLE STICK

**Description:** A Spode "Tower" pattern chamber candle stick, c.1825. This pattern was taken from a published work *Views of Rome and its Vicinity* by J. Merigot and R. Edwards, 1796-98, and is entitled "Ponte Salaro." This type of candle stick was meant to be held when a person was moving through the house in the dark. The design meant that the hot wax would drip into the vessel rather than onto their hands. This shape of candle stick is quite a scarce form.

**Size:** 5.25" (13cm) wide, 2.5" (6.5cm) tall.

**Marks:** Blue printed SPODE.

# WEDGWOOD WATER LILY POTPOURRI

**Description:** A stunning Wedgwood "Water Lily" pattern three-piece potpourri vase, c.1815. This pattern was introduced in 1808 and underlines Josiah Wedgwood's keen interest in horticulture. Potpourris tend to be quite rare, as they are often delicately potted and prone to damage. It is especially rare to find the inner lid still with the piece as a whole. This lid was put in place to seal in the potpourri's aroma, and was removed when the scent was required. You can just imagine that the lids were put "in a safe place" and were never returned to the potpourri.

**Size:** 12" (30.5cm) tall, 6.5" (16.5cm) wide.

**Marks:** Impressed WEDGWOOD.

# Partial Smoker's Set

**Description:** A partial smoker's set, c.1825, printed with the ever-popular view of "Nuneham Courtenay, Oxfordshire," which is also known as the "Wild Rose" pattern. It was taken from an engraving by W. Cooke, published 1 February, 1811. The view depicts Nuneham Park House on the left, which was the seat of Earl Harcourt. A smoker's set was intended to cater for every need of the smoker. It usually had a tobacco jar, ashtray, goblet, candle stick, various pots and snuff boxes (see further example later in this chapter). The goblet and candle stick are missing in this case. Note the multitude of small boxes in this example, some of which are writing related. The set includes a sander, an ink well, a central screw-top box, and other boxes. These sets were sometimes referred to as the "Bargee's Companion."
**Size:** 6" (15cm) tall, 8" (20cm) wide.
**Marks:** Unmarked.

# Blue Printed Flask

**Description:** A blue printed pottery circular flask, c.1835, printed to the centre with a European-like scene which has two men punting in a boat before a large castellated building. The border is identical to Wedgwood's "Blue Rose" border. These flasks were used to carry a variety of liquids and are usually referred to as pilgrim flasks. They are an uncommon item of transferware.

**Size:** 6.5" (16.5cm) in diameter, 8" (20cm) including the spout.

**Marks:** Unmarked.

# Spode Musicians Candle Extinguisher Tray

**Description:** A Spode "Musicians" pattern double candle extinguisher stand, c.1820. This scene of village musicians is just one print from seven scenes that make up the "Musicians" pattern. This stand would have originally had two conical snuffers that would be used to extinguish a candle (see another example later in the chapter with one remaining snuffer still in place).

**Size:** 5.25" (13cm) wide, 2" (5cm) tall.

**Marks:** Printed and impressed SPODE.

# Circular Inkwell

**Description:** A circular inkwell, c.1840, printed with three romantic panels of a girl picking flowers in a landscape. The inkwell has three outer holes for the storing of quills and a central and removable ink vessel. This might have been a blue printed pot originally.

**Size:** 3" (8cm) wide, 2" (5cm) tall.

**Marks:** Unmarked.

# Greyhound Quill Holders

**Description:** A pair of Staffordshire recumbent greyhound quill holders, c.1840-60, both printed with the standard "Willow" pattern border around the bases. While greyhound quill holders are not uncommon, examples with a blue printed border are scarce. This treatment is more commonly seen on cow creamers of this date. Quill holders were, as the name suggests, to hold writing quills. These figures were designed to go on a desk, where they would have been an essential as well as an extremely decorative part of a gentleman's writing equipment. Although these quill holders are outside the dateline of this book, they are interesting and unusual enough to deserve inclusion.
**Size:** Both 7.5" (19cm) long, 5.5" (14cm) tall.
**Marks:** Unmarked.

# Wedgwood Hyacinth Bulb Vase

**Description:** A Wedgwood "Botanical" series hyacinth bulb vase, c.1815, printed with four different botanical specimens. Josiah Wedgwood took these from the 'Botanical Magazine', by William Curtis and was first introduced in 1810. A hyacinth bulb was placed in the bulbous shaped section at the top of the vase. Water filled the lower section of the vase and the hyacinth's roots would grow down into the water. Despite the wide foot, these vases are rare survivors, as they were prone to tipping over.

**Size:** 10.25" (26cm) tall, 5.75" (14.5cm) wide at the foot.

**Marks:** Blue printed W.

# Spode Desk Stand

**Description:** A Spode desk stand, c.1825, printed with a scarce pattern called "Star Flower." The stylish Spode sheet pattern is often highlighted with either enamels or gilding and it is uncommon to see it without either of these treatments. The desk stand has a dished pen tray, a moulded and integral candle stick, a removable lidded ink well, and a removable sander (non-matching in this example). Pottery desk stands are incredibly rare pieces, but were an essential accessory for the well-to-do Georgian gentleman.

**Size:** 8.25" (21cm) long, 3.5" (9cm) tall.

**Marks:** Blue printed Spode.

# Davenport Jug & Cover

**Description:** A very unusual Davenport jug and cover, c.1825, printed with a wrap-around rural scene from the "Mare and Foal" series. This particular scene is of a rural landscape that includes several houses and cows before woodland. The item has a most unusual cover. When removed, it doubles as a cup with a handle. The handle covers the spout when in use as a lid. This shape in transferware is almost unheard of. It allowed the user to pour measured amounts of liquid into the cup and take a drink. This may have been designed for an alcoholic beverage of some sort.
**Size:** 7.25" (18.5cm) tall, 6" (15cm) wide.
**Marks:** Unmarked.

# Bough Pot & Cover

**Description:** A bough pot and cover, c.1815, printed with a pattern called "Elephant and Statue House" and was possibly made by Swansea. This pattern has a man riding an elephant through a chinoiserie landscape. The bough pot is also printed with six floral sprays which is also a typical Swansea trait. It has a removable cover which has three moulded pottery trumpets which allowed floral specimens to be shown off and displayed. It could also have been used to plant bulbs in and have them grow through the funnels.
**Size:** 8.5" (21.5cm) wide, 5.5" (14cm) tall.
**Marks:** Indistinct blue dot workman's mark.

# Pair of Spode Candle Sticks

**Description:** A pair of Spode "Caramanian" series candle sticks, c.1810, both printed with a view of "Colossal Sarcophagus near Castle Rosso." The Spode engravers used as a source taken from *Views in the Ottoman Empire* by Luigi Mayer, c.1803. Candle sticks are scarce and pairs are even more so in a pattern such as this. This type of candle stick was designed to sit on a table or mantelpiece to provide candlelight in the dark. It is easy to forget just how important candle sticks were in the age before electricity.

**Size:** 8.25" (21cm) tall, 5.5" (14cm) wide at the base.

**Marks:** Blue printed Spode to each.

# Lanercost Priory Water Cistern

**Description:** A very curious water cistern, c.1825, printed with a view of "Lanercost Priory, Cumbria" and this pattern has been attributed to Enoch Wood. Note how the usual border (long leaves and star-shaped flowers) has been replaced with a "Wild Rose" border. The cistern may have had a lead liner originally and would have been used as a watering aid in horticulture. It has also been suggested, however, that it was used as part of a waterfall closet.
**Size:** 21.25" (54cm) long, 7.5" (19cm) wide, 7" (18cm) tall.
**Marks:** Unmarked.

# Snuff Box

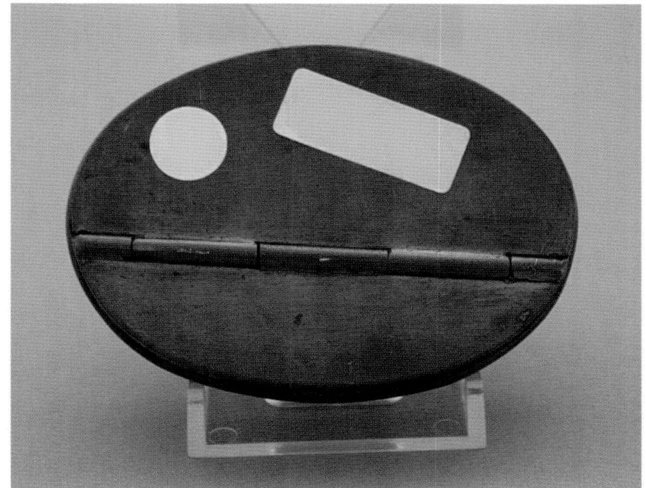

**Description:** A snuff box with hinged pewter cover, c.1840, printed with a scene of a boat on a lake before a castle in a wooded foreground. It has floral sprays around the central cartouche. Snuff boxes are rare items in transferware. At this period, snuff had become the tobacco product of choice among the elite and as such, snuff boxes were a popular and essential accessory.
**Size:** 3.5" (9cm) long.
**Marks:** Unmarked.

# Spode Flower Specimen Vase

**Description:** A Spode "Queen Charlotte" flower vase, c.1817. This pattern name is said to originate from a service made for Queen Charlotte when she visited the Spode factory in 1817. There is, however, no evidence to support this claim. The vase has a flat, removable lid which has fifteen holes pierced in it. They were used to support floral and botanical specimens for display purposes. This was an age of great awareness of one's surroundings, in which a fascination with horticulture played a huge part.
**Size:** 4.75" (12cm) tall.
**Marks:** Unmarked.

# Set of Two Furniture Lifts

**Description:** A set of two furniture lifts, c.1825, printed with various sections of the "Village Church" pattern. Furniture lifts were used to raise pieces of furniture up from the floor. This would stop the feet of an oak dresser getting wet and rotting when a stone floor had been washed. These lifts are extremely rare as they are so prone to damage from both the furniture and people washing and cleaning the floor. Note that they all have a single, pierced draining hole in the top so that they would not retain moisture, which would defeat their object.
**Size:** 3.25" (8cm) tall, 3" (7.5cm) wide.
**Marks:** Unmarked.

# SPODE CARAMANIAN POTPOURRI

**Description:** A Spode "Caramanian" three-piece potpourri, c.1810. It is beautifully printed with "Colossal Sarcophagus near Castle Rosso" to the body, "Sarcophagi and Sepulchres at the head of the harbour of Cacamo" to the pierced lid and "Ancient bath at Cacamo in Caramania" to the inner lid. The Spode engravers used a source from a published work entitled *Views in the Ottoman Empire* by Luigi Mayer, c.1803, for these patterns. Potpourris were used to scent a room with a mixture of spices and floral fragrances. This was especially important at a time when personal hygiene and residential plumbing were not at their most developed!

**Size:** 10" (25.5cm) tall, 9" (23cm) wide.

**Marks:** Blue printed SPODE.

# Willow Bird Feeder

**Description:** A "Willow" pattern bird feeder, c.1810. The "Willow" pattern is one of the most widely used and copied designs in the whole history of transferware. This scarce bird feeder was used to allow a caged bird to take a drink of water. They are called "feeders" and it was thought that they were for feeding caged birds seed, but this is impractical and it is much more likely that the contents would have been water. The open end would be carefully placed through the bars of a bird cage so that the pet bird could take water when it wanted.
**Size:** 5.5" (14cm) tall, 4" (10cm) long.
**Marks:** Unmarked.

# Blue Printed Tiles

1.

2.

3.

4.

5.

**Description:** Five different patterned Spode and Copeland and Garrett tiles: **1.** a Spode "Italian" tile, c.1825, with a green printed SPODE mark; **2.** a Spode "Lucano" tile, c.1825, which is unmarked; **3.** a Copeland & Garrett "Aesop's Fables" tile, c.1835, printed with the "Fox and the Grapes," with a printed C & G mark; **4.** a Copeland & Garrett "Lange Lijsen" tile, c.1835, with printed C & G mark; and, finally, **5.** a Copeland & Garrett "Waterloo" tile, c.1835, that is impressed C & G. Tiles are very rare survivors as they were made to be cemented onto walls and they are either still in situ or were broken in trying to remove them.

**Size:** All 5.25" (13.5cm) square.

**Marks:** C & G, Late Spode and SPODE.

# Eastern Scenery Spirit Barrel

**Description:** An "Eastern Scenery" pattern spirit barrel, c.1825. This pattern of cows watering in an eastern landscape has been attributed to Enoch Wood, although this example has a chinoiserie border rather than the standard floral pattern. Notice how the printer has carefully put a print of a cow on the end of the flask. Spirit barrels were probably for storing spirits, but more in a display role rather than a travelling capacity.
**Size:** 4.5" (11.5cm) tall, 3.25" (8cm) wide.
**Marks:** Unmarked.

# Circular Flask

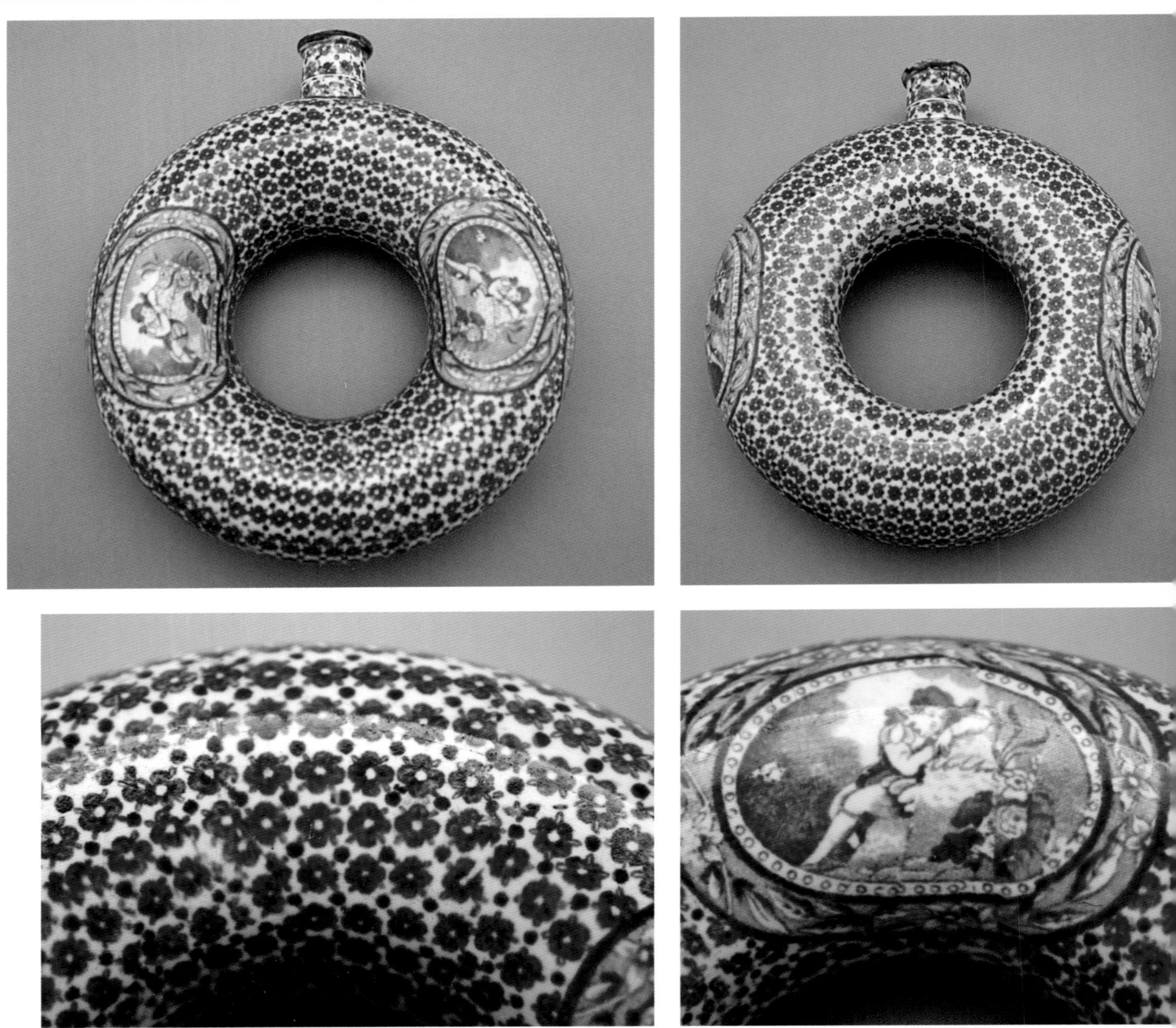

**Description:** A very unusual circular flask, c.1825, printed with repeating cartouches of a sitting boy within a floral sheet pattern background. This shape of flask is most unusual, as most flasks of this size and date are disk-shaped and do not have the central hole. This very tactile flask was probably for water or even spirits and would have had a cork stopper. This pattern has tentatively been attributed to Clews.

**Size:** 7" (18cm) wide, 8" (20cm) including the spout.

**Marks:** Unmarked.

# Beemaster Garden Seat

**Description:** A "Beemaster" pattern garden seat, c.1825, decorated with two different sizes of print taken from the painting *Swarm of Bees, Autumn* by George Robertson (1742-1788). Garden seats were copied from the Chinese versions and were prone to damage due to their size and the fact that they were often used outside. Note the cut-out in the top to allow a hand to be placed inside so that it could be easily picked up and moved around.
**Size:** 19.25" (49cm) tall.
**Marks:** Unmarked.

# Inkwell

**Description:** A floral pattern inkwell, c.1820, well printed with a floral design that has been attributed to Bovey Tracey. The inkwell has four holes around the outside to store quills and a central funnel which allows access to the ink. Inkwells were an essential part of equipment for anyone who wanted to write a letter in the days before fountain pens were in widespread use.
**Size:** 3" (7.5cm) wide, 2.75" (7cm) tall.
**Marks:** Unmarked.

# Small Potpourri & Cover

**Description:** A small "Bird's Nest" pattern potpourri and domed cover, c.1825, printed with a charming scene of a boy showing a bird's nest full of eggs to a girl. Although this example is unmarked, it is attributed to John Dawson & Co., Low Ford Pottery, South Hylton, Sunderland. This elegantly shaped potpourri has two moulded handles and a conical pierced lid. Potpourri contained a variety of dried and natural plant materials to provide gentle fragrances in the house.

**Size:** 5.75" (14.5cm) tall, 4.5" (11.5cm) wide.

**Marks:** Unmarked.

# Spode Tower Dog Bowl

**Description:** A Spode "Tower" pattern dog bowl, c.1825. This was taken from a published work *Views of Rome and its Vicinity* by J. Merigot and R. Edwards, 1796-98, and is entitled "Ponte Salaro." A dog bowl was used as a feeding vessel for dogs or cats. They are considered uncommon today because of two factors. Firstly, there were probably not many made. Secondly, the intended use meant that they didn't survive the experience very well; being "chased" around a stone floor by a hungry canine was not good for longevity.

**Size:** 8.5" (21.5cm) long, 4" (10cm) tall.

**Marks:** Blue printed SPODE.

# Village Church Pattern Candle Stick

**Description:** A "Village Church" pattern candle stick, c.1820, well printed with the four key elements from this famous pattern: the church, the cottage, the sheep, and the men in conversation. Candle sticks are scarce items, perhaps because they were often knocked over in the poor light they provided.
**Size:** 4.25" (11cm) tall, 4.25" (11cm) wide at the foot.
**Marks:** Unmarked.

# Tertial Flower Vase

**Description:** A Tertial flower vase, c.1815, printed with a pattern called "Malayan Long House," with a swan on a lake on the other side. It has a border that is very similar to that used by Rogers on their "Elephant" pattern. The vase has moulded acanthus leaf details around the three trumpet-shaped openings at the top. Vases like this came with a single aperture, three apertures (as seen in this example), and five apertures. They were used for displaying floral specimens in the house.

**Size:** 6.75" (17cm) tall, 6" (15cm) wide.

**Marks:** Unmarked.

# Spode Pyramid Incense Burner

**Description:** A Spode pyramid-shaped incense burner and cover, c.1820. The chimney of the burner is earthenware and is printed with a "Chinese Flowers" pattern variation. The distinguishing factor between the standard pattern and this variation is that some of the flowers and leaves are filled in with blue. The base is porcelain and bears the pattern number 967. Incense burners were used for burning a variety of perfumes and spices to produce a sweet smelling aroma.
**Size:** 4.5" (11.5cm) tall, 3" (7.5cm) wide.
**Marks:** Red painted SPODE.

# Bough Pot & Cover

**Description:** A bough pot and cover, c.1815, printed with a pattern called "Chinoiserie Ruins" which was produced by at least five different potters. It shows two figures in conversation before a ruined building. The pot sits on three bun-shaped feet and has a removable cover. The cover has eight circular holes which would allow botanical specimens to be displayed within the house. This was at a time when people were really beginning to take a great interest in their surroundings including wildlife, nature, and horticulture.
**Size:** 7.75" (19.5cm) wide, 5.25" (13.5cm) tall.
**Marks:** Unmarked.

# Spode Tower Pattern Candle Extinguisher Tray

**Description:** A Spode "Tower" pattern double candle extinguisher stand, c.1820. This was taken from a published work *Views of Rome and its Vicinity* by J. Merigot and R. Edwards, 1796-98, and is entitled "Ponte Salaro." This stand would have originally had two conical snuffers that would be used to extinguish a candle, and, surprisingly, one still remains. Although one has been lost, it never ceases to amaze when tiny items such as the extinguisher, seen here, don't get lost, damaged, or separated from their trays!

**Size:** 5.25" (13.5cm) long, 2.75" (7cm) tall.

**Marks:** Impressed SPODE 47.

# Encrier/Standish/Desk Set

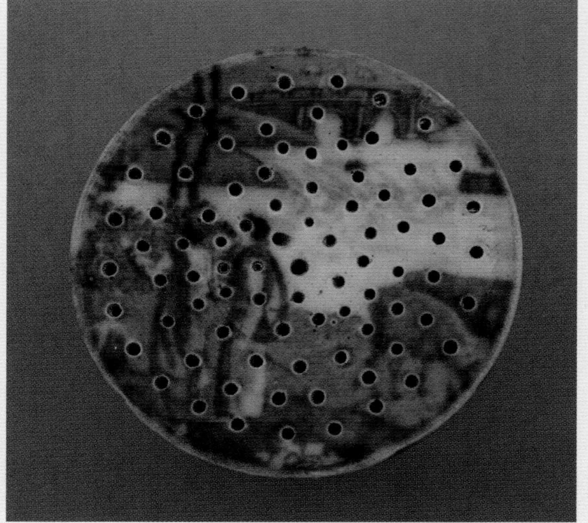

**Description:** An encrier/standish/desk set, c.1820, well printed with the "Philosopher" pattern within a "Wild Rose" border; it is attributed to Robert Hamilton. The pattern shows a man in full flow, perhaps philosophising, gesturing to a reclining woman and two passers-by. This set has a square table-like stand with three holes in the top. There are two surviving pots with this example, a sander and an ink well. The other missing pot was possibly a candle stick or an additional inkwell for another colour ink. These sets were an essential accessory for the well-to-do Georgian gentleman.

**Size:** 9.5" (24cm) long, 4.25" (11cm) tall.

**Marks:** Unmarked.

# Spode Candle Stick

**Description:** A Spode "French Flat" candle stick, c.1825, printed with the "Lange Lijsen" pattern which was taken from a Chinese original. This uncommon shape has a lovely detail, where the potter has made a slit in the side of the stick so that it was easy to remove a spent candle. Often candle sticks are damaged around the flared top of the stick, where people have used a wide variety of objects, some sharp and some not, to remove a spent candle. This design was to stop this from being necessary.
**Size:** 6.75" (17cm) wide, 3" (7.5cm) tall.
**Marks:** Blue printed SPODE.

# Broseley Pattern Bird Feeder

**Description:** A "Broseley" pattern bird feeder, c.1810. This pattern was taken from an original Chinese design. This scarce bird feeder was used to allow a caged bird to take a drink of water. Although they are called "feeders," it is much more likely that the contents would have been water. The open end would be carefully placed through the bars of a bird cage.

**Size:** 5.25" (13cm) tall, 4.75" (12cm) long.

**Marks:** Unmarked.

# Smoker's Set

**Description:** A complete smoker's set, c.1820, printed with a pattern of chicken-like birds and their young before a cottage and windmill. This pattern has been tentatively attributed to Shorthose. This set is made up of seven constituent parts: a candle stick, goblet, ashtray, plate, tobacco jar, press, and snuff box. These sets were sometimes referred to as the "Bargee's Companion." They are quite uncommon, perhaps because they were prone to being damaged. If you consider the height of this example and how unstable it looks and combine this with two other factors that come with the smoker's set, a goblet that is for alcohol and a candle stick that is used in semi-darkness, damage seems inevitable.
**Size:** 13" (33cm) tall.
**Marks:** Unmarked.

# BIBLIOGRAPHY / RECOMMENDED READING


Copeland, R. *Spode's Willow Pattern and Other Designs after the Chinese Strand.* London: Cassell, 1980.

Coysh, A. W. *Blue and White Transfer Ware 1780-1840.* Newton Abbot, Devon: David & Charles Ltd., 1970.

———. *Blue-Printed Earthenware 1800-1850.* Newton Abbot, Devon: David & Charles Ltd., 1972.

Coysh, A. W., and R.K. Henrywood. *The Dictionary of Blue and White Printed Pottery 1780-1880 Vol. I.* Woodbridge, Suffolk: Baron Publishing, 1982.

———. *The Dictionary of Blue and White Printed Pottery 1780-1880 Vol. II.* Woodbridge, Suffolk: Baron Publishing, 1989.

Coysh, A. W., and F. Stefano, Jr. *Collecting Ceramic Landscapes.* Litchfield Street, London: Lund Humphries Publishers, 1981.

Drakard, D and P. Holdway. *Spode Transfer Printed Ware 1784-1833.* Woodbridge, Suffolk: Antique Collectors' Club Ltd., 2002.

Griffin, J. D. *The Don Pottery 1801–1893.* Doncaster Museum, 2001.

Halliday, R. *Pickle Dishes & Milseys: A Social & Historical Commentary.* Northamptonshire: Halliday Publishing/ TCC, 2010.

Hyland, P. *The Herculaneum Pottery.* Liverpool: National Museums, Liverpool; Liverpool University Press, 2005.

Little, W. L. *Staffordshire Blue.* Portman Square, London: B. T. Batsford Ltd., Publishers, 1969.

Moore, N. *Spode Greek.* Petworth, West Sussex: Moore Publishing, 2010.

Priestman, Geoffrey H. *An Illustrated Guide to Minton Printed Pottery 1796-1836.* Sheffield, UK: Endcliffe Press, 2001.

Shaw, Simeon. *History of the Staffordshire Potteries.* Hanley: G. Jackson, Printer & Bookseller, 1829.

Snyder, J. B. *Historical Staffordshire.* Lower Valley Road, Atglen, USA: Schiffer Publishing Ltd., 1995.

———. *Romantic Staffordshire Ceramics.* Lower Valley Road, Atglen, USA: Schiffer Publishing Ltd., 1997.

Spode Society. *The Review.* A bi-annual publication.1986-onwards.

Tanner, A., and G. Tanner. *Swansea's Cambrian Pottery, Transferware & other Welsh Examples.* Stowmarket, Suffolk: Polstead Press, 2005.

———. *Swansea's Cambrian Pottery, Transferware II, Patterns & Borders.* Polstead Press, Stowmarket, Suffolk, 2008.

TCC Database. "Transferware Collectors Club Database of Patterns." www.transcollectorsclub.org

Williams, S. B. *Antique Blue & White Spode.* North Audley Street, London: B. T. Batsford Ltd., Publishers, 1943.

Williams, P., and M.R. Weber. *Staffordshire Romantic Transfer Patterns.* Jeffersontown, Kentucky: Fountain House East, 1978.

# Index

Published by Granada Publishing 1984
Granada Publishing, 8 Grafton Street, London W1X 3LA

Text © Granada Publishing
Illustrations © Colin Hawkins

British Library Cataloguing in Publication Data
Hawkins, Colin

The granny book.
1. Grandmother – Juvenile literature
I. Title
306.8′7 HQ759.9

ISBN 0-246-12434-2

Printed in Italy by New Interlitho, Milan

All rights reserved. No part of this publication may be reproduced, stored in a retrieval system, or transmitted, in any form or by any means, electronic, mechanical, photocopying, recording or otherwise, without the prior permission of the publishers.

# THE Granny BOOK

C000063309